DATE DUE

MAY 0 9 2011			

Top Careers in Two Years

Manufacturing and Transportation

Titles in the *Top Careers in Two Years* Series

1 Food, Agriculture, and Natural Resources
2 Construction and Trades
3 Communications and the Arts
4 Business, Finance, and Government Administration
5 Education and Social Services
6 Health Care, Medicine, and Science
7 Hospitality, Human Services, and Tourism
8 Computers and Information Technology
9 Public Safety, Law, and Security
10 Manufacturing and Transportation
11 Retail, Marketing, and Sales

Top Careers in Two Years

Manufacturing and Transportation

By Rowan Riley

Ferguson Publishing
An imprint of Infobase Publishing

Top Careers in Two Years
Manufacturing and Transportation

Ferguson
An imprint of Infobase Publishing
132 West 31st Street
New York, NY 10001

ISBN-13: 978-0-8160-6905-7
ISBN-10: 0-8160-6905-0

Library of Congress Cataloging-in-Publication Data

Top careers in two years.
   v. cm.
   Includes index.
   Contents: v. 1. Food, agriculture, and natural resources / by Scott Gillam — v. 2. Construction and trades / Deborah Porterfield — v. 3. Communications and the arts / Claire Wyckoff — v. 4. Business, finance, and government administration / Celia W. Seupal — v. 5. Education and social services / Jessica Cohn — v. 6. Health care, medicine, and science / Deborah Porterfield — v. 7. Hospitality, human services, and tourism / Rowan Riley — v. 8. Computers and information technology / Claire Wyckoff — v. 9. Public safety, law, and security / Lisa Cornelio, Gail Eisenberg — v. 10. Manufacturing and transportation — v. 11. Retail, marketing, and sales / Paul Stinson.
   ISBN-13: 978-0-8160-6896-8 (v. 1 : hc : alk. paper)
   ISBN-10: 0-8160-6896-8 (v. 1 : hc : alk. paper)
   ISBN-13: 978-0-8160-6897-5 (v. 2 : hc. : alk. paper)
   ISBN-10: 0-8160-6897-6 (v. 2 : hc. : alk. paper)
   ISBN-13: 978-0-8160-6898-2 (v. 3 : hc : alk. paper)
   ISBN-10: 0-8160-6898-4 (v. 3 : hc : alk. paper)
   ISBN-13: 978-0-8160-6899-9 (v. 4 : hc : alk. paper)
   ISBN-10: 0-8160-6899-2 (v. 4 : hc : alk. paper)
   ISBN-13: 978-0-8160-6900-2 (v. 5 : hc : alk. paper)
   ISBN-10: 0-8160-6900-X (v. 5 : hc : alk. paper)
   ISBN-13: 978-0-8160-6901-9 (v. 6 : hc : alk. paper)
   ISBN-10: 0-8160-6901-8 (v. 6 : hc : alk. paper)
   ISBN-13: 978-0-8160-6902-6 (v. 7 : hc : alk. paper)
   ISBN-10: 0-8160-6902-6 (v. 7 : hc : alk. paper)
   ISBN-13: 978-0-8160-6903-3 (v. 8 : hc : alk. paper)
   ISBN-10: 0-8160-6903-4 (v. 8 : hc : alk. paper)
   ISBN-13: 978-0-8160-6904-0 (v. 9 : hc : alk. paper)
   ISBN-10: 0-8160-6904-2 (v. 9 : hc : alk. paper)
   ISBN-13: 978-0-8160-6905-7 (v. 10 : hc : alk. paper)
   ISBN-10: 0-8160-6905-0 (v. 10 : hc : alk. paper)
   ISBN-13: 978-0-8160-6906-4 (v. 11 : hc : alk. paper)
   ISBN-10: 0-8160-6906-9 (v. 11 : hc : alk. paper)
   1. Vocational guidance—United States. 2. Occupations—United States. 3. Professions—United States.
   HF5382.5.U5T677 2007
   331.7020973—dc22

                                                                        2006028638

Produced by Print Matters, Inc.
Text design by A Good Thing, Inc.
Cover design by Salvatore Luongo

Printed in the United States of America

Sheridan PMI 10 9 8 7 6 5 4 3 2 1

This book is printed on acid-free paper.

Contents

How to Use This Book   *vii*

Introduction   *ix*

Chapter 1 **Quality Manager** 1
Chapter 2 **Distribution Manager** 10
Chapter 3 **Aerospace Technician** 19
Chapter 4 **Aircraft Mechanic** 28
Chapter 5 **Dock Supervisor** 37
Chapter 6 **Air Traffic Controller** 45
Chapter 7 **Machinist** 54
Chapter 8 **Robotics Technician** 62
Chapter 9 **Chemical Technician** 71
Chapter 10 **Laser Technician** 79
Chapter 11 **Microelectronics Technician** 87
Chapter 12 **Plastics Technician** 95

Appendix A: Tools for Career Success   *103*

Appendix B: Financial Aid   *111*

Index   *121*

How to Use This Book

This book, part of the *Top Careers in Two Years* series, highlights in-demand careers for readers considering a two-year degree program—either straight out of high school or after working a job that does not require advanced education. The focus throughout is on the fastest-growing jobs with the best potential for advancement in the field. Readers learn about future prospects while discovering jobs they may never have heard of.

An associate's degree can be a powerful tool in launching a career. This book tells you how to use it to your advantage, explore job opportunities, and find local degree programs that meet your needs.

Each chapter provides the essential information needed to find not just a job but a career that fits your particular skills and interests. All chapters include the following features:

- "Vital Statistics" provides crucial information at a glance, such as salary range, employment prospects, education or training needed, and work environment.

- Discussion of salary and wages notes hourly versus salaried situations as well as potential benefits. Salary ranges take into account regional differences across the United States.

- "Keys to Success" is a checklist of personal skills and interests needed to thrive in the career.

- "A Typical Day at Work" describes what to expect at a typical day on the job.

- "Two-Year Training" lays out the value of an associate's degree for that career and what you can expect to learn.

- "What to Look For in a School" provides questions to ask and factors to keep in mind when selecting a two-year program.

- "The Future" discusses prospects for the career going forward.

- "Interview with a Professional" presents firsthand information from someone working in the field.

- ❧ "Job Seeking Tips" offers suggestions on how to meet and work with people in the field, including how to get an internship or apprenticeship.

- ❧ "Career Connections" lists Web addresses of trade organizations providing more information about the career.

- ❧ "Associate's Degree Programs" provides a sampling of some of the better-known two-year schools.

- ❧ "Financial Aid" provides career-specific resources for financial aid.

- ❧ "Related Careers" lists similar related careers to consider.

In addition to a handy comprehensive index, the back of the book features two appendices providing invaluable information on job hunting and financial aid. Appendix A, Tools for Career Success, provides general tips on interviewing either for a job or two-year program, constructing a strong résumé, and gathering professional references. Appendix B, Financial Aid, introduces the process of applying for aid and includes information about potential sources of aid, who qualifies, how to prepare an application, and much more.

Introduction

Manufacturing and Transportation

Not many people know what they want to do for a living by the time they hit high school. Even fewer end up following their first ideas from childhood. Otherwise the world would be filled with heroic firemen, famous dancers, pro basketball players, and little else. So if you're waffling, wondering whether this or that career would be a good fit, join the club.

School counselors often advertise that computers are the way to go—after all, jobs in that field record the highest growth and good salaries—but not everyone feels attracted to that line of work. Most of us need to use computers and the Internet, but we don't all want to be computer specialists.

To complicate career planning, the jobs we know most about are those done by parents, guardians, relatives, or neighbors—the people in close social circles. However, there is a whole world of employment beyond that. The ways of making a living and creating something special with your life are nearly limitless. At some point, it all comes down to the fact that you are the only one who knows what is best for you. The trick is finding work that matches your personal skills.

Now that's easy to say and harder to do; but keep that point foremost in mind as you look at the wide world of jobs and perhaps feel confused. You can find a way to be happily employed, and it might be in a position you know very little about at the moment. You can make a difference just by offering your skills to a worthwhile effort on a daily basis.

You absolutely need to give the matter some thought. You are encouraged to become actively involved in the process immediately; but take some courage. Remember that no matter what you do at first, you can always make adjustments.

Enough, now, of the cheerleading section: Let's get down to business and make a game plan. You wouldn't be reading this if you were not serious about finding something that's right for you. To that end, this book looks at two very vital fields: transportation and manufacturing. Both economic sectors promise stable job growth. Considering the work involved can lead you toward other fields as well.

Making a Go in Transportation and Manufacturing

This volume looks closely at representative careers in the transportation and manufacturing sectors. Other books in the series consider other kinds of jobs.

You can use these books to "try on" different jobs—to imagine yourself doing the work. Or you can utilize the series for pointed reference, searching for specific information about the kind of coursework you should be completing to align with a certain career—for instance, that of a laser technician.

You can undertake all of the work featured here with a two-year associate's degree. The reason for this concentration is quite practical. Associate's degrees provide essential training needed to pursue a rewarding career path without the expense of a four-year degree. This is a path that many successful people have taken. More than 6.1 million students had enrolled in two-year degree-granting learning institutions by 2005, according to the U.S. Department of Education's National Center for Education Statistics. The number of associate's degrees awarded to graduates continues to increase each year.

In addition, some of the fastest-growing jobs in transportation and manufacturing—in fact, in the country—require only associate's degree training. Experts project that just 23 percent of jobs in the 21st century require a four-year degree (Bankrate.com). And do you know what else? Many of the jobs that require only a two-year degree, such as that of automobile body worker, machinist, or surveyor for construction, are relatively secure, even when the economy takes a downturn.

Transported by Your Skills

The transportation-related jobs featured in the first six chapters can be divided into two categories: those that have to do with vehicle creation and repair and those that have to do with the trafficking of goods and vehicles.

You don't have to be the proverbial rocket scientist to see the benefits available from employment in transportation. This sector includes everything from highway construction to passenger-car rental, from shipbuilding to, well, being a rocket scientist. In 2006, the U.S. transportation sector accounted for $1.4 trillion. The sector employs 16 percent of all workers and makes up a bit more than 10 percent of U.S. economic activity, according to Plunkett Research.

The volume of supplies being moved from place to place is expected to increase 70 percent, as projected from 1998 to 2020, says the U.S. Department of Transportation. There will not be a lack of related jobs anytime soon.

People are especially needed to get products and materials from place to place, in what's known as the "supply chain." "There is a lack of supply-chain people right now; supply-chain management is the topic, and transportation is part of the field," says Tom Craig, of LTD Management, a supply chain management consulting firm. "Given the need for people, there should be opportunities. I would say that anyone entering the field should learn [the] international [side]."

Besides offering basic and stable employment, there are personal benefits to be had from transportation sector jobs. "If you like to travel, there are
definitely travel opportunities within [an area called] logistics," says George
Yarusavage, of Atlas Air. "You're going on site visits to companies that are
moving your freight. If you work for a carrier, you would probably get to
move around the country."

Many of the positions in transportation are easily filled by people with
two-year degrees. To a large degree, the nuances of work in supply-chain
management, vehicle maintenance, and other transportation jobs are
learned on the job; overtraining in school often makes little difference in
the long haul.

"The hiring prospects for [for someone with] an associate's degree who
is trying to get into the supply chain is at least equal to the prospects of [a
similar person with] a four-year degree," says Yarusavage.

Targeted technical training will often do more for you than will a wide-
ranging four-year degree. "I'm trying to get people to go to tech schools to
get technical training," says Al Koller, executive director of SpaceTEC, an
umbrella group of schools in which the federal government provides training for the U.S. space program. "There is probably nothing more important, nor more urgent, than the need to inspire new 'hands' for future
technology work."

Technically Speaking

The majority of manufacturing jobs featured in the second half of the book
are those of technicians. Technicians keep the world running. They work in
many specialties, assisting with business as usual and with the next big
things. Engineers and scientists rely on technicians for their aid, creativity,
and precision. Technicians work between the designing scientist or engineer and the people on the floor. They have, perhaps, the most compelling
job of all: helping to bring theory to life in the real world.

The team nature of research and development and manufacturing has
elevated the technician within industry. Roles and responsibilities blur. The
best person for the job is the one who does the work. That means that you
can enter industry today knowing that hard work and knowledge are what
matter over time. You do not need a doctorate to participate in important
manufacturing improvements. Scientists and engineers now must do so
much paperwork and sit in so many meetings, some technicians end up
taking the lead on projects.

Nowadays, even jobs that are not considered technical require computer and technical skills. Any related training you receive in classes and on
your first jobs will roll over into other fields, should you find yourself on
another path somewhere down the line.

Jesse Allen does workforce development for Intel Corporation, the
world's largest computer-chip maker, based in Oregon. He often funnels

people into programs that offer a microelectronics degree, and he does so with no anxiety about their future prospects, should they have to move to an area in which manufacturing computer chips is not an option. "This degree gives you an in," he says. "It's based in electronics, so they can go off and do basic electronics."

The other great plus of all of these fields is that they recognize the need for continuing training and an updating of your knowledge base. Technicians learn to roll with the rapid changes in their fields, and that makes them ideal employees. Brandon Dunlevy has been guiding an education program in Pittsburgh, Pennsylvania, aimed at training area technicians in robotics in order to build a magnetic levitation train, the first of its kind in the country. He says the skills his techs learn will translate to many industries.

"In addition to knowing the robotics . . . they learn about 3-D modeling," says Dunlevy. "We expect they will be able to use their skills outside the project."

As we have become more reliant on technology, we have come to recognize the integral role of technicians. With increased automation, with the advanced technology built into more products within homes and businesses, specialized know-how is needed more than ever.

Technical careers often require only two years of postsecondary training. So it is a fast track to the work world. Competitive souls can continue to add coursework and certifications to keep pace with advancements, both in the world at large and the personal sphere.

An Affordable Route

Paying for an associate's degree to get you started in these lines of work can, at first glance, seem to be beyond your means. So let's break it down to see what the costs end up being. Statistics from the College Board show that the average annual tuition and fees for 2005–2006 at a four-year private college were $21,235, while the annual cost at a public two-year institution averaged $2,191. And financial aid is not just for four-year college students—those attending trade, technical, vocational, two-year, and career colleges can also qualify for aid. The College Board reports that grant aid averages about $2,300 per student for those attending two-year public colleges. Schools that offer federal financing must be accredited though, and the U.S. Department of Education provides a list of accredited institutions at www.ope.ed.gov/accreditation/index.asp. The money is there.

Just as with four-year students, two-year students who want a piece of the aid pie usually must file the Free Application for Federal Student Aid (FAFSA). Lenders are increasingly helping the two-year student as well. SallieMae (http://www.salliemae.com) offers very specific private loans for career training, and U.S. Bank just introduced the CampUS Education Loan specifically aimed at students attending two-year schools.

Many students who start with a two-year degree end up continuing with higher education later, even while on the job—pursuing a four-year degree and often transferring credits earned from their two-year program. Some go on to earn a more advanced professional degree. There is built-in flexibility, and the classes are like money in the bank.

Another great feature about associate's degree programs is that admission is not overly competitive. Students are admitted from a wide range of academic backgrounds. So someone who performed below average in high school can excel at a two-year school if he or she puts in the time and energy.

Highest Paying Jobs Commonly Held by Those with an Associate's Degree

Heating, Air Conditioning, and Refrigeration Mechanic
Electrician
Telephone Installer/Repairer
Electrical and Electronic Equipment Repairer
Data Processing Equipment Repairer
Registered Nurse
Police/Detective
Dental Hygienist
Radiologic Technician
Electrical and Electronic Technician
Designer
Medicine and Health Manager
Engineering and Related Technician
Drafter
(Source: Bureau of Labor Statistics)

Powered by an Associate's Degree

Compared with workers who hold only a high school degree, associate's degree holders earn more money ($2,000 to $6,000 a year more on average) and face a much lower rate of unemployment. It is also a fact that 43 percent of four-year college grads are underemployed. That means, in some instances, that they might be taking jobs at fast-food chains when they are schooled in foreign relations or art history. On the other hand, there's a shortage of people with technical skills, including those trained at the two-year level.

Two-year training has grown much more extensive and diverse over the past 10 years. Associate's degrees are available not only in more traditional fields such as health care, accounting, and programming but in cutting-edge areas such as e-mail commerce, nanotechnology, the culinary arts, and computer animation.

Flexibility has been one of the main attractions of two-year degrees. Classes are often offered at night, and many programs are now taught via the Internet. Still, those looking for the more traditional college experience will find that at least 20 percent of two-year colleges provide housing, cafeterias, sports, clubs, and a bustling social scene.

Also, because associate's degree programs are very occupation-oriented, students spend a lot of their time getting "hands-on" experience. They either work on-site at actual businesses or perform practical exercises in the classroom that give them real-world experience. For example, students at the Art Institute of Pittsburgh helped design a bicycle that scientists could use in Antarctica—drawing up blueprints and creating a prototype. This real-world experience is often a prerequisite for landing an entry-level position, and many internships and apprenticeships lead directly to full-time employment.

Begin Right Now

So remember, the prospects in transportation and manufacturing look good. A two-year degree can get you where you need to go—and there are multiple ways to pay for the training. It is obvious that earning a two-year degree will take you further than not having one, but which field should you study?

As you read on, you'll see that jobs in transportation and manufacturing are intertwined, as are the jobs in all the books in this series. That is the nature of business and employment. We all need one another. Now let's get specific. Very specific. Let's look at career options in these vital fields.

Each chapter that follows looks at one career. The first half of the book considers representative careers in transportation. The second half looks at manufacturing. The selection of careers is by no means exhaustive.

If you like what you read about a job, you might also consider the related careers listed at the end of each chapter. There might be something there for you to study further.

All lists, for schools with related two-year degrees or associations that can provide connections, are meant as starting points for your personalized job search. One thing leads to another.

The most important things to consider about each position include the needed skills sets, education, and abilities, and its core values and future prospects. The more you know about any given job, the better you are able to make a decision about your probability of success doing the work.

The very first chapter is about quality control. The interview subject inspects automotive parts. So is his job in transportation or in manufacturing? It truly is a little of both.

Quality Manager

Vital Statistics

Salary: Median annual income for entry-level workers in the field of quality management is about $28,000, according to 2006 data from the U.S. Bureau of Labor Statistics.

Employment: Although growth overall is projected to decline, according to the Bureau of Labor Statistics, look for growth in regulated fields in which products require multiple inspections, such as pharmaceuticals, and in industries in which mistakes are costly, such as aerospace.

Education: Get a degree in a targeted area, such as aerospace technology. Earn specific quality-control certifications, such as Six Sigma or ISO 9000, as called for within your industry of choice.

Work Environment: You work inside or outside depending on the product.

Think about stacks of blue jeans in a department store or specialty shop. Someone designed the pockets, the zippers, and the cut; but someone else made sure they came out just right. The same goes for the car you drive, right down to tiny plastic pins under the dashboard. Measuring quality is a major part of the production process. In the work world, controlled product inspections are the key to continued success. What's more, the skills learned by quality systems employees often translate from one industry to the next.

The classic manufacturing model has long included hands-on inspection teams with specialized product knowledge, who test and okay the goods created. In many industries, those kinds of duties are now handled by cross-company committees whose members have training in quality-control processes, such as those taught by key programs that go by the names of Six Sigma and ISO 9000.

"Generally, I'd say that a fair portion of the quality improvement efforts taking place in American organizations are being redirected as Six Sigma projects," says Paul Keller, vice president of Quality America.

Six Sigma is an assessment format taught at institutions around the country. It provides specific steps for groups hoping to improve quality. A company will create quality committees, and then, to reap the benefit of multiple viewpoints, include on the committees people from different sectors of the firm. The idea is that creating a shared platform within a company cuts down on communications problems. In addition, a company that adopts these measures often finds that outside partners are working from the same book. It can make things easier when everyone is talking the same talk.

Such programs have a foothold on U.S. industry now. However, some businesses still keep separate quality departments. That is the case when goods are heavily regulated, requiring workers to jump through governmental hoops to prove their products' worthiness—or when items are simply too expensive to goof up. You cannot be in the business of making pharmaceuticals or rockets without inspectors.

Some quality control positions are threatened by automation. Robots can do some of this work, without a need for health insurance. However, in a number of industries, there is no way to automate the final judgments. When product worthiness involves appearance, performance, smell, taste, or texture, people make final calls. A machine can beat up a pair of athletic shoes, but who decides whether the shoes feel okay afterward?

What does that mean for the new graduate? Related jobs, even as they change form, remain available. In businesses competing globally through rapid advances in related technology, there is little time for mistakes and no room for error.

"The future of quality systems [jobs] is actually quite good," says John W. Sinn, professor of applied quality science at Bowling Green State University, in Bowling Green, Kentucky.

On-the-job inspectors say the work offers personal rewards beyond vacation days and compensation. Your job is to question materials, parts, or products. You are also responsible for the equipment used in the manufacturing process. Is it operating safely? Is the speed optimum? For manufacturing inspectors, the company product is not just a concept discussed around a polished board table. Quality technicians and supervisors see how everything gets done. They are first with practical solutions for reducing waste and time, for improving products and workplaces.

On the Job

Quality professionals inspect and test materials and products. Sometimes this means pulling a random sample and taking it to a lab. Other times it means taking a list of inspection points out to the line and testing for each one.

A car engine is entirely different from a painkilling capsule; but as a quality improvement professional, you find that principles of inspection carry across fields. Depending on the product, you're often checking for chemical, electrical, or mechanical properties and in much the same way as your counterpart in another company. An inspector of canned chili looks for color just as an inspector of car seats does. Both kinds of inspectors also play chemist, looking for the effects of heat on the product.

In addition to technical duties, your position requires that you be organized. You spend part of each day at your keyboard, tracking and reporting your findings. You translate data for administrators who do not have a technical background.

You usually find yourself working indoors, although the inspection of some products, such as jets, sometimes requires exposure to the elements. Some work environments, such as fume-filled chemical plants, involve some danger; the manufacturing environment varies.

No matter what you test and quantify, you'll often find yourself near the action, right where materials and products are being produced. The quality supervisor is often part of a management *team*—he or she is on the line, inspecting the material, part, or product, measuring its effectiveness, seeing it through. However, you'll also find yourself removed to testing arenas and meetings.

Let's say you work for a laptop manufacturer and your assignment is a new keyboard. You apply related government safety regulations, such as electronics standards, by recording and evaluating data. You respond to crises: A major laptop producer, for instance, recently recalled batteries that were catching on fire. The batteries had come from another manufacturer. Your input would be called for in related meetings. You summarize findings. Your most important function is *your* final product: a green flag that the keyboard is ready or suggestions for improvements. Either way, the work you do comes to something. It is a foundation on which all the other employees stand.

> ## "Quality is never an accident; it is always the result of intelligent effort."
> —John Ruskin, British writer and critic

 ## Keys to Success

To be successful in quality improvement, you should have

- the ability to motivate and manage others
- attention to detail
- communication skills
- persuasive skills
- math and physics understanding
- mechanical aptitude

Do You Have What It Takes?

If you have an eye for detail and a mind attracted to finding solutions to everyday problems, you have qualities needed in quality control. Are you good with blueprints? Specifications? Your mental powers are called into practice on the job, yet your work is also hands-on. Testing requires mental and physical skills.

You often need manual dexterity, the ability to manipulate things with your hands.

Another part of the job is providing your findings. You will be reporting to superiors in small and large meetings. If you like the spotlight, you will have a chance to shine. If you prefer to stay behind the scenes, you can often let your findings do the speaking for you.

A Typical Day at Work

A day for a quality manager in food might begin with a reading of reports. You might then call or be called into a meeting regarding an upcoming visit from upper management. The team decides what has to be done so that a new line of jarred, cold veggies is ready for inspection and comment. You then have to go to the line to speak with workers there. You tell them what happened at the meeting and talk about their schedule. After lunch, you turn your attention to another product in development; the company is basically repackaging a tomato sauce and cutting some of the sugar in the recipe. You determine that a visit to the related line is needed. Using a checklist developed by your team, you see where you are in the process. Something is off with the label. You confer with the line manager to make a correction. You determine that a certain number of products have become waste material. You wind up the day returning e-mails and calls.

How to Break In

When fulfilling your chosen associate's degree, be it in chemistry, mechanics, or something else, become familiar with your school's job placement services. Pay attention to companies that hire often; some prefer people willing to go through their own educational programs. While in school, look for part-time employment within your targeted industry. Search for internships or work-study programs that give you something to show on a résumé. Join related professional groups, such as the Society of Manufacturing Engineers and the American Society of Mechanical Engineers, to network. The American Society for Quality offers voluntary certification that can help with job advancement.

Keller recommends earning at least a green belt, which is the lower level of available Six Sigma certifications. That way you "will retain a functional role in the organization . . . and contribute [your] process expertise to the Six Sigma team." In other words, if you're a manufacturing inspector with a green belt, you can bring your hands-on knowledge of the product to any Six Sigma team. The certification can help you get ahead.

Two-Year Training

Technical schools with two-year degrees in engineering, chemistry, or the like offer practical classes that help students land related work upon graduation.

Often the theories and practices you need to learn are presented by professors with industrial experience or who are working as engineers. A typical course of study will include basics in English composition, speech, and the humanities, with algebra, trigonometry, calculus, and physics. You might take computer programming, logic control, manufacturing system design, mechanics of materials, statistical quality control, and more. Many schools offer quality control technology as a course of study. You will be given the opportunity to learn about manufacturing processes from all angles. You should leave with a command of computer techniques. Your mastery of technology will prepare you for quality control, management, design, field services, even sales.

What to Look For in a School

Your big break, moving you from the relatively sheltered world of school to the work world, will depend in a large part on the training you choose. Be sure your institute of learning will serve you well. Ask the following:

☞ Do the instructors have ties to the real world?

☞ Is a job-placement team with a good track record available to me?

☞ What kinds of internships are available through the school?

☞ Does the coursework offer enough for my area of specialty?

☞ Is the lab equipment up to date?

The Future

In quality systems, as in just about every other field, the evolution of technologies and changing market realities require that you stay alert to trends. "Quality professionals are traveling more as international trade increases," says Ron Atkinson of the American Society for Quality; so knowing languages can be a bonus for you. The greater use of automated inspection equipment will put an end to related jobs in some industries, especially in heavy manufacturing, such as building trucks. The delegation of inspection duties to assembly workers will further erode the number of openings. However, the business knowledge you acquire in the inspection process will prove invaluable as your career develops. It is your job to see through standard practices and find small creative changes that add up to savings of time and money. These problem-solving skills can be highlighted in your résumé as your world changes. You use analysis. You audit. You can use your know-how to move into other roles in which you identify avenues of improvement. Make shifts as needed—as your interests lead you forward.

Interview with a Professional:
Q&A

Brandon Giles

Quality control manager at Delta Engineered Plastics, Auburn, Michigan

Q: *How did you get started?*

A: I started off in college [Ferris State University, Michigan]. We were required to do two internships. There was a small plastics firm near my home, so I went with that. The president of the firm was very helpful.

Q: *What's a typical day like?*

A: A typical day now is that we're usually running anywhere from four to five [plastics] presses. I deal with a lot of our customers. There's some travel, but not a whole lot. There's a lot of customer interaction. I assist my boss with PPAP [Production Part Approval Process, which helps suppliers meet specifications]. That's required for [work with] automotive companies. . . . The automotive suppliers require certification from their suppliers. It's all about traceability, doing what you're supposed to be doing, and verification of the process. That's quite a bit of paperwork, but I go out to the presses, check the parts out, and talk to the operators. There's not one set thing I do each day. I also supervise the quality technician. He does a lot of the plant-floor duties, like checking parts, which frees me up quite a bit.

Q: *What's your advice for those starting a career?*

A: Just be persistent. If you put your work in, get your résumé right, you'll find work. I think that after I accepted this job, I had four people calling with other work. Probably the most helpful thing was the internship I had.

Q: *What's the best part of quality control?*

A: The thing I like most is that you get to see all the new programs before they're developed and put on the market. Let's say a large automotive company comes in. We may be helping them work on stuff that will be on a 2009 car. You get to see all of that. And I like dealing with the customers. It's a good job with a lot of flexibility and growth possibilities.

Did You Know?

Three strikes and an umpire might be out! Baseball's strike zone illustrates the role of machinery in quality control. Since 2001, Major League Baseball has employed cameras and three-dimensional imaging to evaluate how often umpires judge the zone "correctly."

Job Seeking Tips

Use these suggestions to tailor your job hunt, and turn to Appendix A for additional help.

✔ Zero in on an area that interests you and build a résumé of experience that is directly related.

✔ Reach out to professionals and ask them career-related questions.

✔ Look for a mentor.

✔ Earn certifications that add to your hiring attractiveness.

✔ Know the employer's product.

Career Connections

For further information, contact the following organizations.

American Productivity & Quality Center http://www.apqc.org

American Society for Quality http://www.asq.org

Best Manufacturing Practices http://www.bmpcoe.org

Center for Quality Management http://www.cqm.org

National Center for Manufacturing Sciences http://www.ncms.org

National Institute of Standards and Technology http://www.nist.gov

Associate's Degree Programs

Search online for schools that match your interests. Here are a few to get you started:

Austin Community College, Austin, Texas

Baker College, Cadillac, Jackson, Muskegon, and Owosso, Michigan

Ridgewater College, Willmar, Minnesota

University of Cincinnati-Clermont College, Batavia, Ohio

Financial Aid

These programs fund scholarships in the field of quality systems. For more information regarding financial aid, turn to Appendix B.

American Society for Quality http://asqstatdiv.org/awards.htm

Dale E. Fridell Memorial Scholarship http://www.straightforwardmedia.com/fridell/form.php

E. Wayne Kay High School Scholarship http://www.sme.org

Related Careers

Construction and building inspector, food processing worker, industrial designer, industrial manager, motor vehicle parts manufacturer, occupational health and safety specialist, plastics product manufacturer, technology field service technician, and technology salesperson.

Distribution Manager

Vital Statistics

Salary: The median annual salary for purchasing agents, who may rise to become distribution managers, is about $43,000, according to 2006 data from the U.S. Bureau of Labor Statistics.

Employment: Distribution is the fastest-growing sector of the transportation industry. New third-party companies are handling increased warehousing and distribution needs so that manufacturers can focus on products. Although employment of distribution managers and purchasing agents is projected to grow more slowly than the average for all accupations through 2014, increases are projected for jobs in service-related business, according to the Bureau of Labor Statistics.

Education: College business and computer courses are important for anyone seeking managerial duties. Include international business courses if possible. Consider certification from organizations such as the American Society of Transportation and Logistics.

Work Environment: Distribution managers usually work in an office but are sometimes expected in the field. Distribution centers tend to be built near major highways.

If you could take all the items in your house or apartment and multiply them by the 110 million households in the country, you would wind up with a mind-boggling pile of goods. Despite the enormity of it all, every item made is moved from one place to another, and often, more than once. The flat-screen TV on your wish list traveled from a manufacturing plant to a distribution center to a retail outlet. The food cooling in your fridge left growers in bulk, traveled to packagers and distribution centers, and then sat in supermarkets until you (or a member of your household) carried it home for your consumption.

Distribution is a complicated game of planes, trains, ships, and trucks. Airplanes fly packages for messenger services, including all kinds of items, such as T-shirts ordered over the Internet. Paneled trucks deliver wrapped desserts to convenience stores. On major rivers and seas, ships move train cars filled with everything from motorcycles to cooking oil.

Now, can you picture yourself in an organizing role, making sure items are sent to the right places? You might be responsible for loading ships, making certain government regulations are met and trade laws are followed. With growing markets in Russia, China, and elsewhere, shipping is increasingly important, say experts. You might be filling planes with items on order, or given that the bulk of the nation's supply fulfillment is covered by trucking, it's likely you would be moving around truckloads of goods. However your career might play out, one thing is sure: Transportation distribution can be an exciting field, filled with opportunity to prosper and travel.

"The job prospects are quite good, especially at entry level," says George Yarusavage, manager of indirect procurement at Atlas Air. The supply-chain management field lacks enough young people to fill the future ranks, he says, possibly because the benefits go largely unadvertised. If you're willing to work your way up, there is plenty of opportunity. "Quite often the college grads you get come from marketing or a general discipline—even converted engineers," he says. "So for somebody new to come in with an associate's degree and a sort of specialty in supply chain or procurement, they would do well."

When the U.S. government deregulated trucking in 1980, the distribution field took off. The feds stepped back, and trucking became super competitive. Some manufacturers honed the handling of their own distribution and introduced money-saving reforms. Others could not keep up with that end of the business, which led to the development of a new kind of transportation firm—third-party providers who manage the movement of goods. They are hired by manufacturers who want to be free to concentrate on production. These providers are exactly where many jobs are now: categorizing, stocking, loading, and moving items for companies big and small. These transportation firms are looking for hardworking, detail-minded people who can help them compete here and globally.

Are you a people person who likes to tackle problems? Are you able to analyze data and situations and see your way clear? You might find yourself very happy in management at a distribution center.

On the Job

The work of the distribution manager is to mind the process of moving goods from one place to another. It sounds deceptively simple, but being good at the job is a matter of hard work and smarts. In a supervisory position, you manage the ordering and distribution of products and parts. You keep your eye on the clock and balance money coming in and going out, making sure deliveries arrive in a manner that maximizes sales.

You might be responsible for hiring and evaluating staff, so part of your day probably includes informal visits among them. You need to stay on top of personnel issues. You might spend part of the morning looking over traffic routes, searching for ways to make your assigned routes most efficient. Another part of your responsibilities might include ordering parts and equipment to keep the warehouse operating at peak performance. During the year, you might review office procedures, determine areas of waste, and make changes. You'll need basic competencies in word processing and spreadsheets, such as tracking payroll in Excel. Safety measures might also fall under your concern. The larger the company, however, the more likely it is that safety specialists will be aboard.

In distribution, managers interact with all manner of transportation professionals, from truckers to CEOs. You have to keep up ties with retailers, promising delivery dates and making good on your promises. You open a line of communications with store management, making certain that goods that flowed through your business were received in good shape. Increasingly, it is important that distribution pros work in concert with everyone along the supply chain and are onboard with the jargon and concepts of people working along the line, top to bottom.

> **"I would say that anyone entering the field should also learn international. We import everything now; then we are concerned with distributing it to retailers, etc."**
> —Tom Craig, LTD Management, Logistics and Supply Chain Consultants

Keys to Success

To be successful in logistics and material management you should have

- strong communication skills
- computer and information management abilities
- attention to detail
- an ability to see patterns
- strong product knowledge

Do You Have What It Takes?

To succeed, you'll need to read industry trends and know what forces affect you. You'll view the daily news in a special way; bad weather on the other side of the world can have everything to do with you. You'll need to be able to think both small and large. For instance, you may have to identify the best way to handle a tiny item being shipped and yet maximize efficiency for the total shipment. A distribution manager assesses available information and relies on his or her judgment to make the best call. Although you will often report to senior-level management, you'll be in charge of staff. You'll need strong people skills, particularly the ability to keep your workers motivated.

A Typical Day at Work

You might go into the office, pour yourself a cup of coffee, and sit with the latest field report, detailing recent deliveries and notes from the people who made them. You take feedback from truckers regarding a problem with a route along an interstate that is under construction. You resolve the problem by finding an alternative path after conferring with team members. Then you send out an e-mail memo to alert everyone. You're aware of an increase in tolls along a certain thoroughfare. You determine the cost effectiveness of sticking with the route versus using a longer route and increasing fuel costs.

A clerical helper brings you orders for parts and services that need your approval. Today you need to okay maintenance items for the garage that services your trucks.

Most companies have specific training needs for new hires; so part of your day might involve working with someone new and teaching him or her the ropes. Another part of the day finds you in meetings. You're needed to forecast the flow of work orders, based on past records and what you're hearing about new business possibilities from the sales people. Perhaps you recommend additional trucks and drivers. You are the go-to person for this sort of information.

How to Break In

Earn your associate's degree in business, taking every opportunity to network with people in the field. Look for related part-time work as a way to build a résumé early. Strive to work under people who mentor others. Managers learn important aspects of logistics during on-the-job training, but a college education will assist you as you try to move up the ladder. Make sure you know your way around computers; the skill will serve you well. Take advantage of internship opportunities offered by your school. Be proactive and join related trade organizations and unions for other sources of training and networking. Most people know just the big names in the business, such as FedEx or Swift Transportation. However, most of the jobs are with firms unknown to the general population.

Two-Year Training

An associate's degree in business or transportation management prepares you to apply math concepts to business realities. You'll learn basics such as double-entry accounting in financial accounting classes and basic economics in courses on marketing principles. You will probably take a class in the history of the industry, so you can spot trends. Often, you'll learn international business relations, giving you a foundation of knowledge related to cultural and legal issues. Good schools will make sure you can demonstrate an understanding of geography and know how to employ Global Positioning Systems (GPS) and global information systems (GIS). You'll also be trained in managerial principles: planning, organizing, supervising, and controlling. You will come to understand the fundamentals of safety, along with the basic issues of materials handling and order processing in inventory control. You will often have a class in customer service management, so you know how to measure client satisfaction and to retain business.

What to Look For in a School

Your choice of school can make all the difference as to the opportunities you find when you finish. Before you transfer into a program, ask the following:

☞ Do the teachers have real-life experience in transportation distribution?

☞ Will the school train me in calculations, payroll basics, and accounting principles, including simple and compound interest?

☞ Does the school offer the science of customer service?

☞ Will I come to understand safety issues and be given the tools to understand the regulations?

☞ Is there training in related computer technology?

☞ What is the school's rate of placement for internships and jobs?

The Future

The distribution field looks very strong. There is more consumer demand than ever for shipped goods. Yet fuel costs are rising, so there is a greater need for high-performing transportation managers. Meanwhile, technology informs our every move. The prepared manager takes command of these innovations and uses technology to share logistics information with suppliers and customers. Prospective employers look for bright people with up-to-date training to help them meet the demands of the new century. In the decade leading to 2014, transportation, storage, and distribution management employment is expected to grow 22 percent, according to the U.S. Department of Labor.

Interview with a Professional:
Q&A

Blair Thomas

Manager, Business Process Integration, DSC Logistics,
Des Plaines, Illinois

Q: *How did you get started?*

A: [In college I] took a few classes in something called supply-chain management and logistics. I liked how we weren't studying anything that was too crazy or that couldn't be applied in real life. When I was getting ready to graduate, the thought of going into a sales job just didn't sit well with me. I wanted to use my leadership skills to do something with results I could see. My company was recruiting for their management training program on campus, and I jumped at the opportunity. After I came on, I was managing a shift within just a few months. It was more responsibility than any of my friends from high school had at that point.

Q: *What's a typical day like?*

A: In warehousing, there are few typical days, but you basically walk into a big jigsaw puzzle. On one hand, you have a certain amount of work to do and get done—load X trailers, unload Y, pick Z orders—and on the other you have your workforce—two people out sick, one on maternity leave, one with a sore back, etc. Your job as a manager is to complete the puzzle with the resources you have. It's a job with results you can see, feel, and measure. Throughout the day, you're making decisions all the time, trying to look out for the best interests of the company, the customer, the product, the employees, and yourself.

Q: *What's your advice for those starting a career?*

A: A few things . . . Number 1: Never apologize for ambition. This is an industry with a lot of people who have no desire to move forward. They are good workers but often can be reluctant to accept ideas from a younger person. Number 2: Don't be afraid to make a decision. It's usually better to make a decision with 80 percent certainty now than waiting for 100 percent certainty when it's too late.

Q: *What's the best part of your job?*

A: You don't work in a cubicle, and no day is ever the same.

Did You Know?

The average miles an item is shipped has increased to more than 530, 100 more than a decade ago. Meanwhile, big shippers such as Dell, Home Depot, and J.C. Penney are working on fleets that use less fuel and give off fewer pollutants. Wal-Mart has pledged to double fuel efficiency in the next decade.

Job Seeking Tips

Here are suggestions to follow to find employment within the industry. Turn to Appendix A for advice on résumés and interviews.

- ✔ Be specific about functions you have performed in internships and throughout your early work experience.
- ✔ Figure out which types of industries—say, clothing versus hazardous materials—most interest you, and take related courses when you can.
- ✔ While in school, work in transportation and distribution internships and part-time jobs.
- ✔ Make use of the career placement office and the helpful professionals there.
- ✔ Join related organizations and attend or volunteer at conferences and other meetings.

Career Connections

For further information, contact the following organizations.

American Society of Transportation and Logistics http://www.astl.org

Association for Operations Management http://www.apics.org

Council of Supply Chain Management Professionals http://www.cscmp.org/

LogisticsToday http://www.logisticstoday.com

Warehousing Education and Research Council http://www.werc.org

Associate's Degree Programs

Search online for schools that match your interests. Here are a few to get you started:

Bloomfield College, Bloomfield, New Jersey

Clark State Community College, Springfield, Ohio

Milwaukee Area Technical College, Milwaukee, Wisconsin
University of Alaska Anchorage, Anchorage, Alaska

Financial Aid

Two sources for related scholarships follow. For more on financial aid for two-year students, turn to Appendix B.

Council of Supply Chain Management Professionals
http://www.cscmp.org

StraightForward Media Business School Scholarship
http://www.straightforwardmedia.com/business-school/

Related Careers

Administrative services manager, buyer, claims manager, inventory control analyst, rate analyst, storage manager, terminal manager, transportation representative, and warehouse supervisor.

Aerospace Technician

Vital Statistics

Salary: Aerospace engineering and operations technicians earn a median salary of more than $52,000 annually. Manufacturing workers in aerospace average $1,019 weekly, according to 2006 data from the U.S. Bureau of Labor Statistics.

Employment: Jobs for engineering technicians are expected to grow as fast as average, according to the Bureau of Labor Statistics. Becoming educated in a quality aeronautics or aerospace program is the key to getting ahead in this field.

Education: Various associate's and bachelor's degree programs in aerospace or aeronautics fit the bill. Interested high school students should concentrate on math and science courses.

Work Environment: Most technicians work full time in a laboratory or at a plant. Some exposure to equipment and toxic hazards is possible, but not inevitable.

The movie *Apollo 13* follows U.S. astronauts into their homes and the outer reaches of the sky. Tense drama occurs among ground-control personnel when the astronauts' lives become endangered. The film is a partially fictional account based on real events.

Since its start, the space program has provided narrative more dramatic than many screenwriters could invent. The heroes of these space stories would seem to be the astronauts, with all the risks they assume as they leave Earth. However, there are countless team members who make those moments—those incredible forays—possible. The know-how of untold numbers of technicians bears upon the outcomes and successes of our human endeavors in the skies beyond.

International cooperation is now making it possible for the United States to build and maintain the International Space Station, an accomplishment shared with Brazil, Canada, the European Space Agency, Japan, and Russia. The station already provides a home for rotating teams of astronauts. When completed, it will weigh more than 1 million pounds. On other fronts, NASA is involved in several long-term space projects, including an unmanned trip to Pluto and beyond.

Behind these space projects is an army of trained technicians. Areas of opportunity for technicians within the space industry range widely—from aircraft to guided missiles to space propulsion units. Entry-level specialists are called for at all stages: assembly, coating, electronics, fabrication, machining, welding, and more. You install and maintain launch equipment.

You determine the cause of malfunctions. Within your specialty, you utilize testing equipment to monitor and keep vehicles on track. Your hands-on training with complex computer and communications systems helps you record and interpret important data. You sometimes assist scientists in research, design, and development. Often, your knowledge is put to use in quality-control functions. You are called upon to repair items of vital importance.

Within the aerospace industry, anything that has to be built—or rebuilt—needs people to construct and test it. The opportunities for aerospace technicians go far beyond the space program too. Techs can be involved in the manufacture of army helicopters or commercial airliners. They may help find an improvement for an unmanned defense vehicle, built to rove the skies. Their work might benefit the Defense Department or a telecommunications company with satellites.

Someday soon, aerospace technicians will be called upon to service the International Space Station. "It is only a matter of time," says Al Koller, executive director of SpaceTEC, an educational partnership that is training technicians with NASA's support. "As soon as you can add someone, you are going to send someone who can repair things and calibrate things."

Not everyone with related training will reach space, but your diagnostic skills can take you into many fields that help people: avionics and aviation, computers, telecommunications, the biomedical field, and more. "I tell people that few communities have rocket launch pads," says Koller, "but every community has a medical clinic." Perhaps there is a trip to great places in your future, based on a career in the aerospace field.

On the Job

Every system used for flight and space exploration is part of the technician's realm. The design and manufacture of each spacecraft's parts, small or large, require the dedication of countless workers. You might find yourself working on communications equipment. You might specialize in navigational needs. Your area of expertise might end up being launch systems. Perhaps you become part of the team that lands the vehicles. Every day, you will wake up and put your practical knowledge and attention to detail to work for you and your employer. You will diligently apply your specialized skills, tackling one piece of sophisticated equipment after another.

Each day is a practical expression of training in math, science, and engineering principles. You might spend time bent over pages of data. You might find yourself examining a prototype for a new part; but all your days, together with those of your teammates, represent our country's effort to send the best vehicles into space. Lives depend upon it.

Consider these major points of the aerospace technician Code of Conduct, a guide to on-the-job conduct: Improper actions, poor quality performance, or the use of unapproved technical processes under any conditions are not acceptable.

It is each technician's responsibility to apply common sense and "best practice" techniques in decisions where specific rules do not provide all the answers.

On the job, you make a difference in the success or failure of flight. So you must work expertly and responsibly. It is expected of you. NASA-bound or not, you will likely receive from any aerospace firm you join the training to keep you up-to-date with changing technology. So think of taking classes as part of the job description, and prepare yourself to stay on top of further advancements.

Are you ready? Let's count down what it takes.

> ### "Space is for everybody. It's not just for a few people in science or math, or for a select group of astronauts. That's our new frontier out there, and it's everybody's business to know about space."
> —Christa McAuliffe, the first teacher in space,
> who died in the *Challenger* explosion

Keys to Success

To be successful as an aerospace technician, you should have

- science skills
- teamwork ability
- attention to detail
- ethics and sense of self-responsibility

Do You Have What It Takes?

Maybe you're the student who took the assignment to build a small toy car and ended up enjoying the project immensely. Perhaps you tinker with electronics, small machines, or large engines in your spare time. If you're a hands-on kind of person with an interest in space and with math and science aptitude, this might be the field for you. Have you always liked figuring out how things work and why? Do scientific principles interest you? Do you have a strong grasp of basic math principles? Are you happy working as part of a large team for an effort much greater than yourself? You have the qualities needed to become an aerospace technician.

A Typical Day at Work

At its most basic, a day as a technician might involve the assembly of the fin of a space shuttle or the wing of an airplane. More than a third of aerospace workers are directly involved in production. Hundreds of assemblers work together during different parts of the process to create a single craft. In a typical day, you might examine a set of instructions or engineering specifications and follow through to assemble your assigned section.

The machinists are those techs who build parts too small to be created in mass. Again, your day might involve the study of blueprints and specifications and the effort to make the plans come to life. Those in tool-and-die jobs might be reading electronic blueprints and operating computer-controlled machines to form tools and molds. Meanwhile, the quality inspectors perform numerous safety checks and measuring performance. The manager and directors make sure the teams interact appropriately.

As a technician, you might also find yourself involved in some aspect of computer-aided design. So your day might involve a meeting or two, consisting of engineers, technicians like you, and even the customers, be they military brass or private owners. You may be required to offer your opinions and input, and your responses will be taken seriously.

How to Break In

Both become and represent yourself as a lifelong learner. Take high school classes that support the core curriculum of aerospace technology: math and science. In college and thereafter, indicate your willingness to upgrade skills as needed. If blueprint reading is missing in your background, take related classes. If computer skills need polishing, sign up. The industry's biggest customer is the U.S. military and its subcontractors. Familiarize yourself with the needs of the branches of the military. Not everyone with this specialized training will end up at NASA in Florida or Texas; jobs ebb and flow with the support or lack thereof from current government administrations. So be ready to apply your skills to the military or private sector. Join aerospace associations and take related part-time positions or internships while in college to make contacts with people who can help you land a job.

Two-Year Training

An associate's degree in aerospace technology readies you for employment in aerospace and related industries. In well-regarded schools, you will be given hands-on preparation and training with related equipment in materials and processes classes. Your laboratory preparation is perhaps the most important, providing the skills and confidence you need to make the right decisions about equipment and perform with optimum understanding. Classes in aerospace safety, applied mechanics, and electrical principles will be balanced by a core curriculum of math, humanities, and communications. You will be trained to work as part of a team and required to produce only at the highest level of quality and safety control. Your main concern should be the school's job-placement rate. See where grads go before you decide to apply to any particular school. Look for SpaceTEC schools in your college search; those schools have programs endorsed by the government through funds from the National Science Foundation. Their classes are developed with input from the space program and target NASA's needs now.

What to Look For in a School

The more closely connected a school is with the aerospace industry, the more frequently graduates will be placed in good jobs. Ask these questions:

☞ Will the college's labs mimic those of an actual working environment?

☞ Is there state-of-the-art manufacturing equipment for practice sessions?

☞ Is there appropriate training in computers and computer-operated equipment?

☞ What services does the career planning and placement office offer?

☞ What industry credentials do the instructors have?

☞ What diversified skills will students learn to help them land related jobs, in case NASA and aeronautics opportunities are limited at the time of graduation?

The Future

According to the U.S. Bureau of Labor Statistics, employment in aeronautics and aerospace product and parts manufacturing is expected to grow 8 percent through the decade leading to the year 2014. What affects that figure most are the changing fortunes of the aircraft business. Fewer new planes were ordered after air travel dipped following the 2001 terrorist attacks on the United States. Several air travel companies experienced bankruptcy. However, current demand for military aircraft and missiles is high.

Another factor to consider is the average age of aerospace workers. Engineers and technicians flocked to the industry in the 1960s, after President John F. Kennedy declared the race for space would be won by the United States. They will be reaching retirement in bulk, increasing opportunities for younger workers. Relatively few NASA workers are under age 30.

Interview with a Professional:
Q&A
Diana Kiesling

NASA quality assurance inspector, Cocoa, Florida

Q: *How did you get started?*

A: I loved reading science fiction. I was fascinated with things about the future—all the gadgets. So this is just great for me. I began taking classes at the Brevard Community College in Cocoa, Florida. The program I enrolled in is called Aerospace Technology and is a two-year associate's of science degree. This was a fun program because it was more hands-on than [it was] sitting around listening to a teacher lecture. We built a large aluminum tool box for the Structures class and a composite wing for Structures II. I learned how to solder and build fiber optics cable. I launched a model rocket for Technical Task Analysis class. I began working as a quality inspector for NASA [through SpaceTEC recruiting] and was hired on full time after I graduated.

Q: *What's a typical day like?*

A: A typical day at the office consists of working on space flight hardware. When the technicians perform work on the shuttle's external tank, solid rocket booster, or orbiter, the quality inspectors are there to make sure the work is performed to the directions listed in the operations manual. It's like working on your car and having a Chilton's or Haynes auto manual. Well, the space shuttle has one too. When an engine is removed and put back in, inspectors are there to help the technician out by making sure the directions are understood.

Q: *What's your advice for those starting a career?*

A: Going to college and/or enlisting in any branch of the military service can help you get on with NASA. They are firm believers in the [SpaceTEC] program. You can get more details by going to the NASA Web site.

Q: *What's the best part of your job?*

A: The best part of my job is spending time out at the launch pad. This is where everything comes together, including the astronauts. Everyone is in a great mood right before launch. It's very exciting.

Did You Know?

The International Space Station will be 361 feet long when it is completed. That's as long as a football field, including the end zones. Eight miles of wire will complete the station's electrical system.

Job Seeking Tips

Follow these tips for aerospace technicians, and turn to Appendix A to read about ways to fine-tune your résumé and score at an interview.

✔ Decide which area of expertise most appeals to you and take related classes.

✔ Select a program with a good job-placement rate.

✔ Form a bond with the crew in your school's career placement office.

✔ Try to get related work while still in school.

✔ Familiarize yourself with the wealth of information at the back of this book.

Career Connections

For further information, contact the following organizations.

Aerospace Industries Association http://www.aia-aerospace.org

American Institute of Aeronautics and Astronautics: Student Chapter http://www.aiaa.org

Federal Aviation Administration http://www.faa.gov/education

International Association of Machinists and Aerospace Workers http://www.goiam.org

Society of Professional Engineering Employees in Aerospace http://www.speea.org

United Automobile, Aerospace, and Agricultural Implement Workers of America http://www.uaw.org

Associate's Degree Programs

Search online for schools that match your interests. Here are a few to get you started:

Antelope Valley College, Lancaster, California

Calhoun Community College, Huntsville, Alabama

Pearl River Community College, Poplarville, Mississippi

Thomas Nelson Community College, Hampton, Virginia

Financial Aid

A few aerospace-related scholarships are listed below. For more on financial aid for two-year programs, check out Appendix B.

American Engineering Association Scholarships http://www.aea.org

Brevard Community College Foundation Scholarships http://www
.brevard.cc.fl.us

SpaceTEC Scholarships http://spacetec.org

Related Careers

Aircraft and avionics equipment mechanic and service technician, assembler, computer programmer, computer database administrator, computer scientist, computer software engineer, engineer, engineering technician, inspector, machine setter, operator, and tender, machinist.

Aircraft Mechanic

Vital Statistics

Salary: Aircraft Mechanics earn a median annual income of about $45,000, according to 2006 data from the U.S. Bureau of Labor Statistics.

Employment: Although major airlines are struggling, they are not the only employers of mechanics, and the general aviation picture is good; the existing workforce is aging. Employment of aircraft mechanics is expected to grow as fast as the average for all occupations through 2014, according to the Bureau of Labor Statistics.

Education: Look for hands-on training that includes newer technologies, such as advanced electronics, then test for FAA certification.

Work Environment: Are you in shape and ready to climb ladders? You will work in hangars and outside.

Now here's a career that can help you soar. If you have mechanical aptitude, you can put your skills to use in the service of jet and non-jet aircraft. Jobs are available and should be for the foreseeable future.

"We have no problem getting people hired," says Fred Mirgle, who oversees the aviation maintenance science program at Embry-Riddle Aeronautical University, in Daytona Beach, Florida.

When people think of aircraft mechanics, they often think of teams of mechanics servicing airliners at airports. A jet pulls up to the gate. Mechanics scurry out in bright work uniforms, with earplugs on. It's obvious that everyone knows exactly what needs to get done and is working on the clock. But working on the line at a big airport is only one way to go with this career; the exacting work of an aircraft mechanic takes many forms.

Some people set up their own shops, attending to small planes with private owners. Still others specialize in helicopters, such as those used by police and medical teams. As a mechanic, you can call the shots regarding where you'll live and what you'll do. There are only so many large, international airports, but there are smaller fields all over the United States and Canada.

You might have the sense that aviation is troubled. The business sections of your local and national newspapers have been forecasting disaster for airlines: Many have failed in recent years. Strikes by airline workers of all stripes have been widely publicized. However, aviation is a wide open field. Not everything that flies is a commuter vehicle taking ticket holders to vacation and business destinations. General aviation companies are looking for talent. The manufacturers of small jets and other aircraft need your mechanical skills too.

The Bureau of Labor Statistics reports that related jobs will be most readily available in smaller companies but that demand looks healthy in general. Look to commuter and regional airlines and in other outlets, such as air cargo transport.

"If you look at what's happening in the airline industry, with all these corporate jets," says Fred Mirgle, "that segment of the business is really doing well."

The economy and air travel have made gains since the international terrorist attacks of 2001 sucked the air out of the business. Meanwhile, the population has been growing. This means more bodies to move from place to place. With the globalization of commerce, additional goods need to be moved from country to country. People with knowledge of aircraft systems are in demand.

The employment picture is also brightening because many master mechanics currently working in the field are reaching the age of retirement and plan to move on. The skills of aircraft mechanics transfer to other fields, so these retirees can look forward to a second act in other repair work, just as you can, should you decide to follow this path. It's a built-in plus of aircraft mechanics. Consider this fact as well: Many young people with the aptitudes needed in aircraft mechanics are going into computers instead; so you just need to zig while they zag.

On the Job

Aircraft mechanics often work out in the elements, in all kinds of weather. The work they do keeps planes in the air and landing safely. The completion of even the most minor aspects of these jobs is important, so staying focused is crucial. However, that's also why you'll experience built-in rewards as an aircraft mechanic: You stay active and keep the public safe.

The work falls into one of four categories. Airframe mechanics are responsible for maintaining every part other than engines, instruments, and propellers. Avionics technicians work on the components used in communications, navigation, weather radar, and the computers controlling the engine and other functions. Aircraft power plant mechanics specialize in the engines and propeller. Then there are the mechanics doing just about everything outside of working on instrumentation. They might specialize in air conditioning, body repair, electrical systems, pneumatic systems, rigging and controls, or plumbing.

These mechanics and technicians work together to make certain that all aircraft have regularly scheduled maintenance required by the Federal Aviation Administration (FAA). Together, the mechanics and technicians make repairs and inspections. They take engines apart, looking for signs of wear and tear. They operate X-rays and other equipment, searching for cracks.

Some specialize in preventative work. They check engines, landing gear, you name it; if there's a defective part, it must be found.

With a specialization, you might find yourself mastering the turbine engine; or you may hire yourself out as an expert in composite materials, someone who can repair surfaces, such as graphite and fiberglass, which are used in new aircraft. There is a host of specialized skills in advanced production and repair. The best way to pick a specialization is to start classes and keep asking questions, letting your special interests lead you forward. With so many ways to take this career, you're sure to find something that flies.

An aircraft mechanic once noted three words on the "problem" line of a report: "Target radar hums." After fixing the problem, the mechanic then wrote: "Reprogrammed target radar with the lyrics."
—from Progressive Engineer.com

Keys to Success

To become successful as an aircraft mechanic, you need

- physical agility, to climb ladders and move in small spaces
- conscientiousness and focus on deadlines
- curiosity, to stay on top of new technology
- diagnostic and troubleshooting skills
- mechanical aptitude

Do You Have What It Takes?

Are you afraid of heights? This job may not be for you. Other than that, what you need to succeed in the field is mechanical aptitude and a great attitude. A good aircraft mechanic is self-motivated and able to tackle problems with an open mind and determination. In order to keep your certification valid, you need to stay working and continually place yourself in refresher courses. You should also be able to get along and work on a team. And the so-called soft skills, such as being able to communicate, orally and in writing, are becoming essential. Companies want employees who can communicate with people and show what they know.

A Typical Day at Work

You are whistling in pleasant weather. Your buddy gathers diagnostic information from the jet's electronic box. The pilot has complained that a gauge isn't working. You use electrical test equipment to sort through related wiring. Sure enough, you locate the problem and order a new gauge from your parts department. (Hopefully it's in stock!) While waiting for the part, you look up the related reference materials: removal, installation, and test procedures. Your supervisor comes across the ramp to find out how much longer it's going to take. You estimate a time. The part arrives, and you cross your fingers that it actually fixes the problem. Inside the aircraft, you look down the aisle and see the passengers looking up at you, some scared, some annoyed. After kicking the pilot out of his seat, you replace the cockpit gauge and make sure everything is working properly. It's finally time to head back, sign off, release the aircraft, and wait for the next big one to roll in. You check your watch: 10 minutes until arrival. You check the computer to see if the pilot wrote up any discrepancies on the next one, and it all begins again.

How to Break In

To work in avionics and instrumentation, you need an associate's degree in electronics and certification from an association such as the Electronics Technicians Association, the International Society of Certified Electronics Technicians, and the National Association of Radio and Telecommunications Engineers. FAA certification is needed for general repair. Otherwise, you will work under a certified aircraft mechanic. Your youth will work to your advantage, because those workers who have studied the newest technologies will do best in coming years. New trade skills are replacing traditional ones. Areas of special interest include advances in composite materials and electronics. Electrical systems are becoming more elaborate. Make certain you have cross-training in multiple aircraft systems, to help keep your options open.

Think about adding some management classes to your résumé. Within the field, there are numerous levels through which to advance: from mechanic through shop supervisor and even onward to the executive level. Nearly half of all aircraft mechanics join a union; look for contacts there as well.

Two-Year Training

A good program gives you plenty of hands-on training. The basics you'll learn in FAA-approved aircraft technology classes, often named by number or level, include electrical and ignition and starting systems, airframe assembly and rigging, induction and air flow systems, and specialties such as composite structures and hydraulic and pneumatic systems. You'll do much of your training in labs and shops. If the school is all talk, it's certainly not what you want.

Whether you plan to specialize in aircraft electronics or not, a good portion of your training should center on electronics and computers. These days, "troubleshooting is becoming much more than just going in with a wrench," says Fred Mirgle. More than ever, he says, you need to know computers, so study microprocessors. Study basic electricity and aircraft electricity, instrument systems, and aircraft electrical systems as well.

Those who serve in the military and receive related training might find that the work experience is enough. Otherwise, look for a school that is FAA approved. In the end, you'll be tested with a series of exams taken by computer and a day with an examiner. Afterward, you're given projects that cover everything from small planes to giant jets.

What to Look For in a School

To make sure your school is not a fly-by-night operation, check whether it has a track record. Ask the following:

☞ Where do graduates land?

☞ Will I learn about microprocessors and interfacing?

☞ Do the avionics classes go beyond electronics theory to offer aviation electronics labs?

☞ How new are the equipment, tools, and labs we will be using regarding navigation and communications systems?

☞ Does the school place students in internships and have allies in local aircraft operations?

☞ What and how current are the instructors' credentials?

The Future

Aircraft mechanics employed by the major airlines tend to be at the top of the earning scale, but gainful employment is available elsewhere. Right now, according to the Bureau of Labor Statistics, more than half of aircraft mechanics and technicians work for air transportation companies. Another 18 percent work for the FAA, many in the main hangars in Atlantic City, New Jersey; Oklahoma City, Oklahoma; Wichita, Kansas; and Washington, D.C. Some 14 percent are employed in aerospace-related businesses. The rest help transport executives and cargo or are self-employed. Make yourself useful to smaller companies by having well-rounded skills. Mastering these modern technologies can help you find work in developing countries like China, should you want to live abroad.

Interview with a Professional:
Q&A

Kari Monaghan

Aircraft mechanic and instructor at Embry-Riddle
Aeronautical University, Daytona Beach, Florida

Q: *How did you get started?*

A: My grandfather should get credit for my initial exposure to aviation as he would take us each year to the EAA Oshkosh Air Show. I ended up being a mechanic by default. I couldn't afford flying lessons, and I really wanted to be hands-on with the aircraft. After [graduating], I went to work for Air-Tran Airways as an apprentice technician. About one year later, I decided to take a position as a radio and electrical technician with United Airlines in Chicago. Following the events of September 11th, I was furloughed and decided to come back to [Embry, earn a masters, and teach].

Q: *What's a typical day like?*

A: A typical day for me within the engine repair station includes inspection of various engine components and accessories during assembly and testing. We receive the engines from the flight line, and the students, supervised by me and by qualified student assistants, go through the complete overhaul process of disassembly, cleaning, inspection/repair, reassembly, and test run. These engines are then returned to service at the flight line. In addition to the lab experience that we lead the students through, I have duties as an instructor, teaching proper overhaul procedures for these reciprocating engines in the classroom environment.

Q: *What's your advice for those starting a career?*

A: I would recommend that anyone considering entering the aviation industry as a maintenance technician seriously consider the impact that this type of career will have on his or her lifestyle. Within the industry, it is very common to be on odd shifts, such as midnights or afternoons, also working weekends, holidays—and overtime is usually required. The benefits of such a position need to be considered as well, though. Normally they will include flight benefits which will allow you to see the world for relatively little money.

Q: *What's the best part of your job?*

A: The best part of my current position is that I get to interact daily with students who will shortly be entering the industry. They are all very enthusiastic about their prospects and excited to be starting a new phase of their lives.

Did You Know?

This job can take you places in more ways than one. Aircraft mechanics—and their immediate families—often fly for reduced fares on their airline as well as other, related carriers.

Job Seeking Tips

Consider these tips for aircraft mechanics and then turn to the Appendix A for help with résumés and interviews.

✔ Find an accredited school from which graduates find gainful employment.

✔ Become familiar with the career placement people on campus.

✔ Try to find student employment or internships that are in line with people in the business.

✔ Join professional groups early. Read their literature and attend meetings.

Career Connections

For more information, contact the following organizations.

Federal Aviation Administration http://www.faa.gov

International Association of Machinists and Aerospace Workers http://www.goiam.org

International Brotherhood of Teamsters http://www.teamster.org

Professional Aviation Maintenance Association http://www.pama.org

Associate's Degree Programs

Search online for schools that match your interests. Here are a few to get you started:

Redstone College, multiple cities   http://redstonecollege.edu-search.com/

San Joaquin Valley College, Fresno, California

Spartan College of Aeronautics and Technology, Tulsa, Oklahoma

WyoTech, multiple cities   http://www.wyotech.com/

Financial Aid

A few related scholarships are listed here. For additional general information on available financial aid, look in Appendix B.

Aviation Distributors and Manufacturers Association Scholarships
http://www.adma.org

Professional Aviation and Maintenance Association Scholarships
http://www.pama.org

Aircraft Owners and Pilots Association Scholarships
http://www.aopa.org

Related Careers

Aircraft technicians, automobile and truck mechanics, electricians, electrical installers, electronics installers, elevator installers, elevator repairers, hydraulics mechanics, pilots, and shipbuilders.

Dock Supervisor

Vital Statistics

Salary: The highest 10 percent of earners who are dispatchers or shipping clerks make $52,000 and $37,000, respectively. Shipping, or dock, clerks earn on average $24,400 a year, according to 2006 data from the U.S. Bureau of Labor Statistics.

Employment: Automation is causing this field to grow more slowly than the average for all occupations through 2014, according to the Bureau of Labor Statistics. Even so, it remains a field where inexperienced people can break in.

Education: Earn an associate's degree in business with a logistics concentration; you can add door-opening certification through the American Society of Transportation and Logistics.

Work Environment: Although machines lift the heaviest items, dockworkers are responsible for physical labor, and some lifting is probable. You usually work in an industrial area near highway, air, or water transport.

Do you like to make things happen? You could put that energy to work in the distribution field, keeping U.S. products on the move. Your favorite sports beverage got to the store by just such an effort. Every day, millions of items move from manufacturers to warehouses and are distributed according to orders made at multiple points in every state and every country. As soon as one job is complete, another fills its place. The work of a warehouse is never done.

Does all that movement make you tired just thinking of it? Hopefully not: Companies are looking for candidates who see personal opportunity there. Warehouses serve retailers needing delivery of shirts shown in the latest sales flier, families awaiting computer equipment ordered on the Internet, and most other forms of order fulfillment. Leadership is needed to provide the safe maintenance of the warehouse, its equipment, its contents, and its staff.

Dock supervisors oversee operations, making sure freight is loaded and unloaded in a timely and ultimately cost-effective manner. You smooth life out for your employees. You ease the way for the business that provides your benefits and salary. Think about how essential that is.

Within the United States, docks most often deal with land-based transport. "There was a point at which the truck industry was consolidating," says Fran Chargar, executive vice president of Logistics Horizons, a distribution firm in Rutherford, New Jersey. "But it's a growing piece in the industry today."

You could be someone behind the scenes, figuring out the best way to truck items in and out. "I think companies today are looking into the logistics area as a way of saving money—you know—cutting costs," says Chargar. "I think it's definitely possible to start out in the logistics field in the warehouse. . . . And you can work for third-party companies. . . . Those are companies that go in and manage the distribution function for the big guys. That's a growing field."

In Illinois, for instance, the governor touts a program called Opportunity Returns. The project is aimed at filling a work shortage in manufacturing and transportation, logistics, and warehousing. State officials project that the state will see a shortage of skilled distribution labor as current workers retire and businesses expand. Over 4,000 jobs will open in manufacturing, and the economy will suffer if those positions stay unfilled. "As in manufacturing, the transportation, logistics, and warehousing sectors are all facing major projected shortages in skilled labor in the coming years," notes the governor's appeal.

Freight forwarding is a bustling business in Chicago, Illinois, where O'Hare International Airport is located. Area colleges and community development groups are jumping in to develop programs that provide occupational training in transportation, warehousing, and logistics. Big businesses, such as United Parcel Service, are offering related classroom and on-the-job training.

This scenario repeats in other states where the manufacturing sector is strong. So what do you think? Can you picture yourself on the move, answering questions, directing a dock? Here's a look at the training that will get you there.

On the Job

Consider the land-based freight industry that deals with truck transport. As a dock supervisor, your job is essentially to move freight. You get goods onto and off of trailers. That seems simple enough, but you have to do so without causing damage, and the particulars of the work can be challenging.

Let's say you supervise 50 dock workers. At any given time, you have a crew that includes new and old employees. Part of your day will involve getting some workers up to speed.

Similarly, there might be 30 trailers at the dock. You need to understand the physical issues confronted by your team during the day. Things have to be moved in a safe and efficient manner. You keep track of the shipments electronically. You can call up the contents on your computer and read the planned routes. You have clerks updating the files, using bar codes. The computer tracks shipments as they make their way from point to point, but the machine needs your input. You use the technology to minimize the distance the items travel. There should be little or no wasted effort.

Needless to say, you're on the run. You might not need to do any physical labor yourself on a given day, but you have to stay on top of things. You can't just sit in the office staring at the screen. Dockworkers concentrate on one load at a time. It is not their job to see a bigger picture. You need to do that for them, keeping them motivated and on task. You need to be there when unexpected events cause problems.

The brass ring is efficiency. Helping you achieve that goal is a world of technology. Computer programs can tell you the best way to place a trailer among those already docked; but you need to be the kind of person who has practical vision yourself.

> **"A manager is not a person who can do work better than his men; he is a person who can get his men to do the work better than he can."**
> —Frederick W. Smith, founder of FedEx

Keys to Success

To be successful in shipping and receiving management, you need
- communication skills
- motivational and other people skills
- software skills
- energy levels
- organizational ability
- problem-solving ability

Do You Have What It Takes?

On the job, you are responsible for the efficient sorting and handling of items. You deliver freight in certain timeframes, setting priorities for the work to be accomplished. To be the best at this line of work, you should develop the ability to communicate clearly with people working for you and with upper management. A strong sense of responsibility will get you through the daily challenges. You should be comfortable setting and accomplishing goals and feel at home at a computer keyboard. You should be an energetic person, someone who can keep the dockworkers happily on task.

A Typical Day at Work

Let's say you run the dock at a superstore, where customers can fill their shopping carts with everything from frozen turkeys to new shoes and socks. You have a small team preparing labels and documents for items being moved to another store. They then move the items to the loading platform, using a forklift. You check their work and direct the loading.

Your receiving clerks are responsible for figuring out whether the orders are right before they are accepted. They record a shipment's contents and the shape of things as they arrive. They use scanners to read the barcodes on the boxes. Your staff includes a new employee whose scanner is on the fritz. You make preparations to replace the scanner and instruct the employee on how to enter the numbers manually. In a shipment of frozen vegetables, several of the cartons seem compromised. You confer with your clerk, and you both decide to write the goods off as damaged.

One of your workers is taking too many breaks. Another isn't taking enough, trying to prove himself as some kind of super worker. You take both aside individually to encourage them to exert the optimum level of effort.

How to Break In

When trucking was deregulated in 1980, warehouse- and distribution-based businesses had to provide new customer services to stay competitive. Some firms started offering manufacturers full logistical services in tracking and moving freight from start to finish. This way, their client companies could concentrate on improving their products. The more you can train for these sorts of logistics skills, the more marketable you'll be. No matter which part of the distribution galaxy you choose to shine in, you need classes in logistics and management. Try to get part-time work or internships that pad your résumé with real-world, related experience. Let the career placement professionals at your school help you.

Two-Year Training

Those who work in distribution say the most important and practical piece of your business education is courses that teach how to navigate computer programs for e-business and logistics.

Another special focus is safety. Laborers work with conveyor belts, forklifts, handcarts, and other sometimes tricky equipment to arrange the materials. Any business program you undertake should include management courses about safety programs and related laws.

Along with basic financial math, communications, and strategic management courses, bulk up on production and operations management, supply chain design, lean production, and logistics. Anything that helps with general management skills will prove helpful as well. You need to motivate people. You need to lead people. You need to keep everyone organized.

What to Look For in a School

The right school can make all the difference. Before you pick your place of education, be sure to ask the following:

☞ Are instructors aware of the latest technologies, such as scanners and voice-activated software used to instruct dockworkers?

☞ What will I have learned about information management by the time I graduate?

☞ What is the career placement office's track record in placing students?

☞ What internships does the school make available?

☞ Do instructors have up-to-date, real-world experience?

☞ Will the teachers be around for advice and counseling?

The Future

The major trend in warehouse distribution today is supply-chain integration. That's "distribution talk" for aligning efforts at all points along the trail. Think of it this way: When all firms involved in production, transportation, and warehousing are using compatible inventory systems, the accuracy level goes up and the number of errors goes down. So advances in technology are smoothing the way for greater efficiency. Satellites allow companies to locate trucks and monitor the performance of their engines. Improvements such as Radio Frequency Identification Services, which includes the use of inventory scanners, and voice control software, ease the supervisor's burden. Jobs in truck transportation and warehousing are supposed to grow 14 percent over the decade leading to 2014. That equals the projected rate of growth for all industries combined! Join related associations and keep studying the newest developments.

Job Seeking Tips

Below are tips for job-hunting in this field. Look in Appendix A for advice related to résumés and handling an interview.

✔ Attend seminars in safety and procedures offered by trade associations and unions to acquire further knowledge and industry contacts.

✔ Ask your instructors for job contacts.

✔ Find related part-time employment while attending school.

✔ Utilize the career placement office to help you secure employment in a firm in which there are people with much to teach you.

Interview with a Professional:
Q&A
Robert Bohaty
Transportation supervisor at *Newsday* newspaper,
Melville, New York

Q: *How did you get started?*

A: I was a part-time truck helper. I worked my way up through all the positions in this department. It gave me a very good perspective. It gives you such a great tool to manage the department. I understand what it takes to get things done.

Q: *What's a typical day like?*

A: The thing is, this particular business is a 24/7 business—and it's 365. We're the people who are responsible for getting the paper out and on the street and on time. The night shift consists of the paper running off [the presses] and our loading it onto the trucks. If there are any problems, like if a truck breaks down, or if a press breaks down, we have to deal with it. Essentially that paper has to be on the street by 6 a.m. I've best heard it described as the most perishable product there is. A lot of pressure is on the supervisors to make sure the paper gets where it needs to go. It becomes instinct after a while. Basically you're dealing with problems. On the day side, you're dealing with problems on runs—stores that call up with problems with deliveries. It's a lot of assuring that the job is done correctly. It's very deadline driven. It's also a union environment. You have special rules you have to follow; the drivers have contracts. The best way to win the game is to know the rules.

Q: *What's your advice for those starting a career?*

A: You need your basics: [the Microsoft Office Suite programs] Excel, Word. You should be well versed in everything with computers. It's a must now. You really need to have computer skills. Be aware of the systems you're going to be using—and anything with people skills, any kind of management training. Take business management. Logistics would be good, so you understand the supply chain.

Q: *What's the best part of your job?*

A: Most satisfying I would say is touching all the bases and making sure everything gets out on time. You're doing the right thing, working to solve problems. When a driver comes up to you with a problem and you help him, he's grateful. It all ties together.

Did You Know?

Ever notice truck scales along an interstate? The weight of goods that U.S. trucks carry grows 2.6 percent annually. By 2015, it will equal 12 billion tons, says the American Trucking Association.

Career Connections

For more information, contact the following organizations.

American Society of Transportation and Logistics http://www.astl.org

American Trucking Association http://www.truckline.com

International Brotherhood of Teamsters http://www.teamster.org

Warehousing Education and Research Council http://www.werc.org

Associate's Degree Programs

Search online for schools that match your interests. Here are a few to get you started:

Chaffey College, Rancho Cucamonga, California

Northeastern University, Boston, Massachusetts

Salt Lake Community College, Salt Lake City, Utah

University of Toledo, Toledo, Ohio

Financial Aid

This list can get you started on your scholarship search. For more on financial aid, look in Appendix B.

Garrett A. Morgan Program http://www.fhwa.dot.gov/education/index.htm

International Transportation Management Association Scholarships http://www.itma-houston.org/scholarships.html

Transportation Clubs International Scholarships http://www.transportationclubinternational.com/scholarships.html

Related Careers

Administrative services personnel; courier; dispatcher; inventory control specialist; postal service worker; shipping, receiving, and traffic clerk; and transportation representative.

Air Traffic Controller

Vital Statistics

Salary: After several years of preparation and training, air traffic controllers earn annual salaries from $58,000 to $140,000, with a median of more than $100,000, according to 2006 data from the U.S. Bureau of Labor Statistics.

Employment: Employment is expected to grow as fast as the average for all occupations through 2014, with the majority of openings coming through the need to replace existing workers, according to the Bureau of Labor Statistics. Almost all controllers work directly for the Federal Aviation Administration (FAA).

Education: Air traffic controllers need at least an associate's degree from an approved FAA air-traffic control school.

Work Environment: Work takes place in the control tower, which is an office of windows and radar screens towering above the runways, or at a ground-level control center within or outside the airport limits.

In smaller, municipal airports, the control tower is often the most obvious feature of the landscape. In large, international airports, these towers are enormous, rising above a sprawling complex of terminals, hangars, runways, and parking lots. When you look up and see the large dark windows, it's not hard to imagine the controllers up there, hands at the controls, speaking into microphones, with lights blinking from the control panels around them. Each blip of the radar screen shows a plane's approach.

From related scenes that have been shown in movies and on TV, most people understand that the essential job of controllers is to make sure those radar blips don't get too close to one another. However, those dramatizations don't show the extensive everyday teamwork involved. Most people will guess that these small offices in the sky are where all controllers spend all their time, but that assumption is false.

The work of air traffic control is broken into sectors, or zones, with each controller monitoring certain aspects of a plane's takeoff, flight, arrival, and taxi. Controllers who work in towers are responsible for the aircraft that take off and land. They also direct the traffic of ground vehicles. The busier the airport, the more these tasks are broken into components.

Some air traffic controllers handle arrivals and departures of planes up to an altitude of 10,000 feet or so. They are based in the airport but not up in the tower. Other controllers are considered area controllers. An area controller is given a specific block of airspace to mind. Teams of these controllers work away from the tower in air route traffic control centers, monitoring the flights of aircraft at higher altitudes. Each center's airspace is organized into multiple but fixed routes.

There are also flight service specialists who work at various regional stations around the country. They don't direct traffic, but they do direct private pilots, telling them about terrain, weather, and suggested routes. Some controllers work in the FAA Air Traffic Control Systems Command Center in Virginia, where they monitor the entire sky, warning en route teams of possible problems and assisting centers having trouble with weather, runways, or traffic overload.

It was the Command Center that forced all planes to land at once on 9/11. Think about the tremendous coordination that took, all that could have gone wrong, and all that didn't. This extreme example of grace under pressure speaks to the professionalism of every air traffic controller and the basic importance of the job.

So, no, not all the work is done in the air traffic control tower; and although the safety of passengers and the aircraft professionals is of utmost concern to air traffic controllers, a big part of their job is simply making sure that the planes move fast and efficiently on all the ordinary days of the year. Controllers organize the planes, their flights, and available land and air space. They guide pilots between structures. They make a huge difference by keeping things normal.

> **"Order everyone to land, regardless of destination. OK, let's get them to the ground."**
> **—Ben Sliney, national operations manager at FAA command center on 9/11, the first time U.S. controllers landed all planes at once.**

On the Job

As a plane departs from its gate, a controller directs the pilot to the right runway. Let's say you are the second controller to deal with the departure. You tell the pilot about local conditions that affect flight: weather, wind, and visibility. Then you check related runway patterns and give the pilot the OK for flight. You are conscious of making your directions clear and concise, but you also try to convey friendliness and team spirit. The pilot acknowledges your instructions and sets off down the runway. As the plane travels, it gains speed. As it takes flight, another controller guides it along the way.

The en route controllers take over. These teams are watching certain airspaces. They make sure the plane glides through without disruption. They check the flight plans of other planes traveling within their assigned space. Sometimes, these coinciding plans call for a flight change.

When the plane leaves that team's space, the team that monitors the next space is warned. All along the way, controllers inform pilots of changes that will affect their flights. Often, these controllers are doing two things at once: directing a plane and sending off weather reports. You've heard of "keeping all the balls in the air." The juggling a controller does involves planes—and lives.

This kind of pressure is not for everyone. The responsibility is awesome; mistakes can result in injury and death. To complicate matters, a controller's schedule covers all blocks of day and night. But for those who can handle the ongoing stress of the work, there is good pay, scheduled rest, and the satisfaction of keeping people safe.

Keys to Success

To be successful in air traffic control, you should posess
- the ability to quickly absorb and use data
- the ability to picture time and space
- communication and articulation skills
- concentration
- decisiveness
- team-building skills

Do You Have What It Takes?

A good controller has highly developed spatial awareness and a head for numbers. You must be a person who can remain calm and flexible under intense pressure. Personal qualities such as these are very important—and not so common.

You also need to be a team player, someone who can communicate well with others and anticipate problems in communications. The language most often used is English, so anyone for whom English is a second language must master it completely.

Controllers undergo tests for physical and psychological health. Certain medications are forbidden for those who do this work. You must see well. You must speak clearly. You must hear well too. You have to keep your act together.

How to Break In

While in high school, join flying clubs and explore related camps and part-time work. Take math and science courses. You will want to enroll in an FAA-approved air traffic control school and make friends with instructors and the people in the career placement center, because their recommendations are going to be critical. The competition for air traffic control jobs is keen, but there are jobs available. Many airports are short on trained staff. After graduation, you will have to pass a pre-employment test, a medical test, drug screening, and a security clearance. If selected, you undergo additional FAA training. Whenever you are sent to a new unit on your first job, you will undergo additional training to learn the specifics of the work involved. So for a while you will be under almost constant supervision. You need to be someone your superiors can count on.

A Typical Day at Work

A pilot radios that her plane is approaching. You are working the radar room, below the tower. An associate has been taking flight plans off the printer and has been organizing them. You look at your copy of the plane's flight plan. You match the plan to what you see on the screen. Everything seems to be progressing as it should. However, the airport is busy right now, too busy. So you tell the pilot to circle. You give specific instructions as to how the plane will fit into the patterns of other aircraft that are circling.

Fifteen minutes later, the plane is approaching the runway; you tell the pilot to contact the tower. She does. At this point, she is no longer your responsibility. She is being handed off to the next controller team responsible for that space. Meanwhile, another pilot is calling for instructions. You help him into a waiting pattern as well. Then it's time for a break. A colleague takes over your post. It is well known that after two hours on the job, the performance of any air traffic controller is reduced dramatically, so you'll take plenty of mandatory breaks throughout your shift, and you'll need them.

Two-Year Training

Officials plan to take the next crop of controllers from FAA-recommended schools only. Check the FAA Web site (http://www.faa.gov) for approved programs. There are more applicants than spots, but if you get in, your chances for employment are very good. Your high school grades and test scores can help you make the cut. (If you choose a school not listed, make certain it guarantees placement in private companies providing service to non-FAA towers.) In college, you'll take flight theory and physics for aerospace sciences. You'll study tower operations and airport planning and operations. You should be given a course in aerospace law. You should take meteorology. Upon graduation, you will be assigned to an FAA facility until all requirements are complete for certification, a process lasting two to four years. You will have yearly physicals and a biannual job performance examination. Then be ready to pick up and move, because officials will place you where they need you. The cut-off age for new hires is 31.

What to Look For in a School

When considering a two-year school, be sure to ask the following questions:

☞ Does this school have FAA approval?

☞ Will there be hands-on training?

☞ What qualifications do the instructors have; have they worked as air traffic controllers?

☞ Will I learn the necessary technical skills?

☞ What is the job placement rate for graduates?

☞ Is the equipment up to date?

The Future

As computer-enhanced radar is further developed, the work of air traffic control will evolve. Forecasters say controllers will gradually shift toward computer systems management. The FAA has been implementing a long-term plan to replace old equipment and bring aboard new technologies and procedures. However, it is unlikely that software will be developed to handle all situational crises. Air traffic controllers will always be called upon to resolve problems and use incoming data to their and everyone's advantage.

Meanwhile the role of air traffic controllers is evolving in other ways. For instance, recently the FAA rescheduled controllers at the busiest airports to require more of them to be at their radarscopes at any given time. Controllers contested the decision, which put a squeeze on break times. As a controller, you may take part in ongoing conversations that will affect the future of the business. The profession is a kind of club.

Interview with a Professional:
Q&A
Tim Davis
Air traffic controller, Colorado Springs Airport, Colorado

Q: *How did you get started?*

A: I joined the navy in 1978 and became an operations specialist. The work entailed plotting on charts, writing backward on Plexiglas, working on radar scopes, and talking on radios. I really enjoyed that, but then I met a guy who was an air traffic controller and got a chance to watch him do his job and thought, *Hey I could do that, and it looks like fun!*

Q: *What's a typical day like?*

A: I normally replace the controller who has worked the longest. I plug in next to that person and get briefed. I'm told what the weather has been like, any indication of equipment outages, and the traffic situation. When I am comfortable that I have "the flick, or mental picture" I tell them, "I got it." They move on, and I sit down. The person I replaced remains a minute to make sure everything is going smoothly. Normally you work in position for and hour and a half to two hours, get a break for 20 minutes, and then return for more.

Q: *What's your advice for those starting a career?*

A: Stay focused on all your schoolwork. We do a lot of spatial work, and geometry is a must. Math is good, and so is physics. I know a lot of you are great at talking on the cell, watching TV, and doing homework at the same time. Believe it or not, that is not necessarily a bad thing. If you're good at multitasking, then you have some of the skills needed.

Q: *What's the best part of your job?*

A: I love sitting down at a scope full of airplanes. It's like sitting down at a puzzle without a picture. You make up the picture in your head and then go to work to produce that same picture on the radar screen. It is a lot like chess. You have to think three or four moves ahead. By knowing where the next aircraft is going to fit, you can have the hole already built for it when it gets there. The best part is twofold: One is knowing I have been able to get someone safely to a destination, and the other is being able to see the fruits of my labor right there in front of me, every minute of every hour of every shift.

Did You Know?

You can see planes fly into airports and follow air traffic control communications online. An audience of fascinated listeners scan airbands and feed what they capture into these aviation networks and blogging groups, creating a rundown of current flights. Use an Internet search engine and the phrase "air traffic control" to find one. Or go to http://www.thetracon.com or http://www.liveatc.net/.

Job Seeking Tips

Here are tips to help you become an air traffic control specialist. For general advice about getting work, turn to Appendix A.

✔ Study current FAA hiring procedures, available on their Web site.

✔ Talk with air traffic controllers through related associations, or even online forums, and ask for advice. Use your favorite Internet search engine and search for the phrase "air traffic controllers."

✔ Become familiar with the requirements for certification.

✔ Steer clear of drugs.

Career Connections

For more information, contact the following organizations.

Air Traffic Control Association http://www.atca.org

Canadian Air Traffic Control Association http://www.catca.ca/

Federal Aviation Administration http://www.faa.gov

National Air Traffic Controller Association http://www.natca.org

Professional Air Traffic Controllers Organization http://www.patco81.com

Associate's Degree Programs

Search online for schools that match your interests. Here are a few to get you started:

College of Aerodynamics, Flushing, New York

Miami-Dade Community College, Homestead, Florida

Minneapolis Community and Technical College, Minneapolis, Minnesota

Purdue University, West Lafayette, Indiana

Financial Aid

Here are several scholarships related to air traffic control. For additional information on financial aid, turn to the Appendix B.

Airport Owners and Pilots Association Scholarships http://www.aopa.org

Air Traffic Control Association Scholarship http://www.atca.org

LeRoy W. Homer Jr. Foundation http://www.leroywhomerjr.org

National Business Aircraft Association Scholarship http://www.nbaa.org

Related Careers

Airfield operations specialist, airport administrator, airport manager, logician, pilot, and traffic control specialist.

Machinist

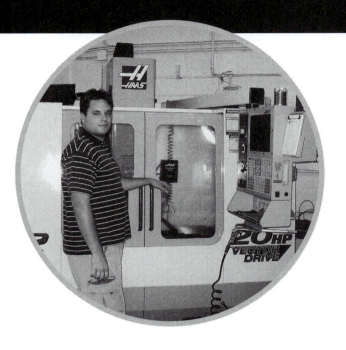

Salary: Machinists make a median annual income of about $34,000, according to 2006 data from the U.S. Bureau of Labor Statistics.

Employment: Partly because of their productivity, machinists face a job-growth rate that is projected to be lower than average for all occupations through 2014; still, openings are forecast to exceed the pool of qualified candidates, according to the Bureau of Labor Statistics.

Education: An associate's degree in applied science, precision machinist manufacturing, or the like provides the foothold needed to gain a position in a manufacturing environment. Continued training occurs on the job.

Work Environment: Employees work in machine areas, often standing and wearing protective goggles to fend off flying metal and earplugs to keep machine noise from damaging their hearing.

Machinists create precision parts by cutting and grinding metal. That sounds pretty basic, but this is work not everyone can do. It takes a special set of skills, a patient mindset, and a can-do attitude.

So how do you know that you're cut out for the work? Ask working machinists. On the Internet forum for Practicalmachinist.com, craftspeople in the field had some fun answering the prompt, "You know you're a machinist when . . . ." One member replied, "You're driving on one of those curved overpasses on the freeway, and you wonder to yourself what the radius of something like that would be." Another said, "You don't return an item that has a missing part. You go out to the shop and make it." Their responses pretty much say it all.

Machinists figure out problems. They are masters of drills, grinders, lathes (which shape materials by turning items against a cutting tool), machining centers, and milling machines (which employ rotating teeth). Machinists have special smarts they apply to all kinds of manufacturing problems. "It's all about troubleshooting," says Marcelo Giuliante, owner and operator of Giuliante Machine Tool Company, in Harrison, New York. It's about thinking mathematically in a very practical way to create or re-create the parts that keep machines moving—that run our manufacturing economy.

Some machine shops produce large quantities of parts. Others develop small numbers of unique items. No matter what their assignment might be at any given time, machinists read specifications, follow directions, and decide which tools they will need to create the correct forms. The job is all about the craft, the exactness. A "little bit off" is not acceptable in this line of work.

In the new manufacturing age, machining is a convergence of automated manufacturing systems and the machinists' knowledge and skills. Machinists have a working understanding of materials and their properties. They are handy with tools. This combination of know-how and adeptness qualifies them to machine items that meet strict specifications. The future is brightest for machinists with capabilities to run CNC machines. Machinists and computer-control programmers work together to plan the steps of the cutting process.

At every level, the job requires planning and follow-through. You read and react to specifications. You determine the best way to create the piece you will need, and then mark and cut the material to form, watching for the changes that heat and vibrations make on the metal. This skill set is needed in small machining shops and large manufacturing firms that produce equipment and machinery, aircrafts and their parts, automobiles and their parts, and steel.

By most measures, the job prospects for future U.S. machinists are quite good, but if you choose this line of work, be careful and keep your wits about you. On the member forum for CNCZone.com, one bored machinist took a poll one day, asking, "Who has a bandage on their fingers?" Replied Big DaddyG: "Fingers?"

On the Job

In the layout stage, machinists read specifications and blueprints. Then they go into planning mode. They determine when to cut into the metal, how fast to feed the metal into the machinery, and how much metal to remove. The process is hot, hot, hot! So machinists must plan for cooling. They then plan the finishing of the piece. They mark the piece to show where additional cuts might be made. They decide how the cuts will be adjusted as the piece cools.

The next stage is called machining. The craftspeople place the metal on the correct tool, whether a drill press or a milling machine, and set the controls so they can make the correct cuts. The machine generates heat as it works on the metal. As part of the monitoring process, the machinist watches the speed of the machine and the heat of the material.

Most metals expand when heated, so the temperature of the material is important to know. The other factor that affects metal is vibrations. Those too must be monitored. Otherwise, the precision of the cuts will be off. The work can be very mechanical, but computerized cutting machines now control much of the cutting. The machinist often works with a programmer to determine the path of the cut and the overall speed of the process—or the machinist acts as a programmer himself or herself. Once the metal piece has been machined, it is checked and measured for quality control. Afterward, machine setters, operators, and tenders finish off the piece.

 ## Keys to Success

To be successful in this field you should have

- ⚷ attention to detail
- ⚷ mechanical inclination
- ⚷ motor skills for detail work
- ⚷ numbers aptitude
- ⚷ powers of concentration and patience
- ⚷ problem-solving skills

Do You Have What It Takes?

Were you one of those kids who took joy in step-by-step building toys? Machinists like reading plans and charts; it seems to come naturally to them, although the skill is actually something that is honed through time. People in this line of work feel comfortable working with numbers and being on their own to get projects completed. They enjoy tackling puzzles and making and fitting parts. They revel in tools and using their hands in their work. What's more, they see and can mark the smallest differences among like objects, so the challenge of precision work is especially appealing to them. They revere quality.

A Typical Day at Work

Machinists will tell you there is no typical day. Everything depends on the projects running through the shop. Private shops often specialize, based on industries in the area. One might be busy making medical parts, such as subcontracting parts for magnetic resonance imaging machines, while another is fulfilling orders of an entirely different nature.

Marcelo Guiliante's shop caters to the aerospace industry. A day depends on the kinds of items being produced, whether they're for flight safety, such as parts for landing gear or the propulsion system, or the nuts and bolts for passenger seats. The machinists with the most experience work independently throughout the day, guiding a part through the planning, marking, and cutting stages. Dull machines make for bad work, so it's not uncommon to spend part of the morning sharpening tools before proceeding. Something simple will take a couple of weeks. Some projects drag into months. Machinists at an upper level might also spend part of the day overseeing the work of newbies on the floor. "In this industry, we have a lot of short production runs," says Guiliante.

How to Break In

It is wise to seek employment within the field, even while at school because many of your skills will be developed while you complete projects. Your work isn't simply academic; you'll have to put your skills into practice. You can earn points as a go-getter by working as a machine setter, operator, or tender during your education. It will also give you an inside track. A vocational school or community or technical college can provide you with the experience and coursework you need to break into the field. Employers who need machinists are often proactive in contacting these schools.

> "The bottom line is, when people want parts, they want parts. . . . If you can get people their blessed parts, they'll go away."
> —James A. Harvey, *Machine Shop Trade Secrets*,
> Chapter 1: "Work Fast"

Two-Year Training

You need classes in math, physics, blueprint reading, mechanical drawing, and quality control and safety practices. Because computers are being utilized more than ever, you need to be trained in the operation and programming of related computerized machine tools. Even then, the ability to excel will come through hours of on-the-job machining. Your school should provide you with plenty of practice with bench work, the lathe, milling, and specialized tools.

National skill standards have been developed by the National Institute of Metalworking Skills. See whether the school's curriculum aligns with those minimums. If you can pass that agency's exam, it will serve you well.

In Canada, you earn a journeyperson certificate after passing examinations and completing certain hours of employment. Your schooling is 8,000 hours or four years, 90 percent of which is work experience in the trade. In the United States, apprenticeships are available through specific unions in certain sectors, such as the automobile industry.

What to Look For in a School

When considering a two-year school, be sure to ask the following questions:

☞ Does the school use the national skill standards developed by the National Institute of Metalworking?

☞ What computer skills will I learn?

☞ Will I get CNC training?

☞ What bench work will there be? Lathing? Milling?

☞ What are the instructors' credentials and practical backgrounds?

☞ What is the school's job placement record?

The Future

New kinds of automation are always being introduced. So be ready to go back for training at intervals throughout your career. Although that might sound discouraging, you should know that the skills you learn as a machinist will not go to waste. Some organizations will reimburse you for the training. New production techniques will call for more workers to be jacks-of-all-trades. Employers need employees who know the process from the ground up. Highly skilled workers will be first in line to run ever-more-expensive machinery.

To advance, think about becoming a CNC programmer, a tool-and-die maker or mold maker, or starting a shop of your own. The most stable machining jobs, through the ups and downs of the manufacturing economy, are those in maintenance and service.

Did You Know?

Hollywood has a take on machinists: the movie *The Machinist* is about a man who stops sleeping and the horror he endures. He is named Trevor Reznik, after Trent Reznor of the band Nine Inch Nails, whose music features heavy machinery sounds.

Job Seeking Tips

Consider these steps toward a machining career. Turn, as well, to Appendix A for advice on résumés and interviews.

✔ Ask instructors for tips on finding jobs.

✔ Use the career placement office at your school.

✔ Get related part-time work or an internship before graduation.

✔ Attend job fairs.

✔ Get prior experience as a setter, an operator, or a tender, the people who set up and tend and operate manufacturing machinery.

✔ Join related associations.

Interview with a Professional:
Q&A

Andrew Meyer

Machinist for National Oceanic and Atmospheric
Administration, Spokane, Washington

Q: *How did you get started?*

A: I originally got turned on to CNC machining and this line of work in high school. My teacher saw that I had talent and pushed me to pursue it. It came very easy to me, and I could see that it interested me. After that, my [technical college] professor—who worked in the field and then started teaching—really helped me get to where I am today.

Q: *What's a typical day like?*

A: A typical day for me: I get to work around 7 o'clock. We usually have a shop meeting. We talk about projects coming up and what we want to accomplish for the week. And once we all know what's going on, we go to work. PMEL [Pacific Marine Environmental Lab] is a small research and developmental shop, not a typical production shop. I get to work one-on-one with the engineers. They will give me a drawing package, steer me in the right direction, and let me fill in the blanks as I go. There is a lot of freedom, and there are opportunities for improvement and for doing many different tasks.

Q: *What's your advice for those starting a career?*

A: I would recommend you first get all the required classes out of the way. That's when you can turn to actual machining classes and labs, then on to programming and computer drafting classes. That's basically drawing 3-D parts on a computer. For any student, I highly recommend a Solid Works or Mastercam class. Every interview I've gone on has asked for experience using these software programs.

Q: *What's the best part of your job?*

A: Every day is different. One day I might be working on the instruments for tsunami buoys. One day I might be working on a boat out on Lake Washington or Puget Sound doing tests on new instruments before we deploy them into the ocean. Some days I could be welding. If you're good with your hands and think a four-year university just isn't for you, community colleges or technical colleges are a faster and just as, if not more, valuable way to get a degree.

Career Connections

For more information, contact the following organizations.

International Association of machinists and Aerospace Workers http://www.goiam.org

National Tooling and Metalworking Association http://www.ntma.org

Navy Metalworking Technology http://www.nmc.ctc.com

Precision Machined Products Association http://www.pmpa.org

Tooling and Manufacturing Association http://www.tmanet.com

Associate's Degree Programs

Search online for schools that match your interests. Here are a few to get you started:

Cuyahoga Community College, Cleveland Ohio

Eastern Iowa Community College, Davenport, Iowa

National Park Community College, Hot Springs, Arkansas

Shoreline Community College, Shoreline, Washington

Financial Aid

This list shows a few scholarships related to becoming a machinist. For more information on financial aid, turn to Appendix B.

Fred Duesenberg Scholarship http://www.mcpherson.edu/technology/history.asp

IAM Scholarship Competition http://www.goiam.org

Jay Leno/Popular Mechanics Scholarship http://www.popularmechanics.com

Randall R. Jones Scholarship http://www.forsyth.tec.nc.us/student/scholinfo.html

Related Careers

Computer-control programmer, computer-control operator, construction worker, gunsmith, locksmith, machine setter, machine operator, machine tender, machine shop owner, metal pattern maker, millwright, stationary engineer, tool and die maker, welder.

Robotics Technician

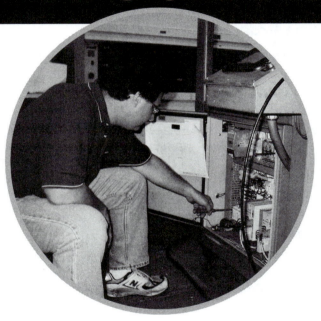

Vital Statistics

Salary: The median annual salary for a technician in robotics is about $41,000, according to 2006 data from the U.S. Bureau of Labor Statistics.

Employment: Overall, job openings are expected to increase as fast as the average for all jobs through 2014, as companies increase their use of robotics to expand productivity according to the Bureau of Labor Statistics.

Education: Earn at least an associate's degree in engineering. Get a solid background in computer numerical control and related technologies to advance in this career; develop your skills with traditional tools as well, such as soldering guns.

Work Environment: You will most likely work inside a manufacturing plant or shop, in a clean area. Some basic safety issues might be stressed, such as the use of goggles.

Robotics can be one exciting ride. Literally. In Pittsburgh, Pennsylvania, robotics students are training to build a magnetic levitation transportation system. That's a futuristic train powered by magnets. It is expected to take riders 300 miles an hour, twice the speed of a regular commuter rail. Students at the Community College of Allegheny County are receiving special training to build the 52-mile track, which will be lined with magnetic fields that will be manipulated by electrical current to move the train along. The robotics students must fabricate over 3,000 beams of steel, to be placed end to end.

These beams cannot be made traditionally, on an assembly line in which the same basic beam is cut over and over. "Because of the need to adjust to the terrain and the speed of the vehicle, each beam needs to be unique," says Brandon Dunlevy, who helps run the project. Each must be perfectly shaped, so electro-mechanical engineering, or robotics, is needed to get the job done.

You don't have to live in Pennsylvania to benefit from the lessons these students are learning. If you open yourself to the pursuit of robotics, you're likely to find all kinds of interesting work. Solar-powered underwater robots now monitor lake water, looking for chemical or biological changes. Robots are sent on shuttles as part of the space program, to explore the surfaces of other planets. Some spas now have robots that give neck massages.

Technicians are part of the design and development process that bring such machines to life.

Electromechanical workers help develop, test, and program new robots, which fit and form all manner of items, from a careful stitch on a patient on an operating table to temperature control and listening devices. Robots are especially well adapted to manufacturing needs, such as forming fuel tanks or moving gigantic truck frames. Using principles of engineering, production, design, and computer electronics, robotics techs benefit their chosen industries.

By its very nature, robotics is involved in cutting-edge projects. Many U.S. manufacturers are updating their production processes to include additional robots even while you read this. For proof of how much these skills are in demand, you don't have to look beyond the train project in Pittsburgh. The area lacked people with the training needed, as does much of the country. Having correctly trained workers was important enough to officials at Maglev, Inc., the train company, that they partnered with the community college to start a two-year program in the specialty. Robotics experts from Penn State and Carnegie-Mellon universities helped develop the curriculum.

For the students, it's a win-win situation. They will take away very marketable skills; they'll earn knowledge and practice hands-on expertise that you could train for as well.

On the Job

Robotics technicians manipulate programmable controllers. So in a way, working can be like playing video games. However, your efforts get real results that make a difference in all kinds of factories, for all kinds of products. These forward-thinking technicians use conventional tools and control systems as well; they do whatever it takes to get the job done.

On the job, you'll use computer programming to your advantage. You'll also use your knowledge of circuits, electronics, hydraulics (operational properties of fluids), general mechanics, and pneumatics (mechanical properties of air and gas), to install and maintain robotic equipment, relying on computers for data. You'll start up and synchronize robots and robotic systems, which do the dirty work of manufacturing. A robotics technician's day revolves around computers, but sometimes you'll pick up a screwdriver or a soldering gun to align robotic components; other times, you'll use a microscope.

A good deal of your efforts will go into inspections, making sure systems are operating correctly and accurately. You'll test and repair robots by reading electrical diagrams and symbols, and you'll report on what you've found.

Trained technicians work with engineers to help in all stages of robotics manufacturing: design and development, installation, operation, and maintenance. Robotics technicians tend to be people with multiple skills who can bring their abilities to bear on a project and offer a bit of creativity now and again. With hard work and a little luck, some move up to supervisory positions.

These skilled workers are needed at robotics manufacturers, suppliers, and distributors. They're called for in industries that rely on robots, such as automotive, aerospace, heavy equipment, and electronics manufacturers, in which hands-on skills and controlled precision are highly valued. Techs are also needed in the apparel, food, and pharmaceutical industries. Chemical, electrical, and petroleum concerns depend on robotics as well. Those are the manufacturers that need robotics most. Just think of the harsh chemicals used in home cleaning products. Many things are best not handled by humans.

> **"The most exciting phrase to hear in science, the one that heralds new discoveries, is not 'Eureka!' (I found it!) but 'That's funny. . . .'"**
> —Isaac Asimov, award-winning science-fiction writer

Keys to Success

To be successful in this field you should be good at

- analyzing problems
- communicating
- focusing at short distances
- manual dexterity and steadiness
- math and logic

Do You Have What It Takes?

Robotics technical work requires concentration and the ability to reason and think creatively. You should be the kind of person who has spatial ability—that knack for seeing how things line up, by dimensions, in your head. If you have what it takes, you are probably aware of your skills already. Are you someone who can figure out steps for putting things together, such as a laminate bookshelf, without much trouble? That's a skill not everyone has and an aptitude that could serve you well in this field. Most of all, working in robotics is hands on; you should enjoy manipulating tools as if it were an extreme sport.

A Typical Day at Work

Let's say you work in a small robotics company that hires out teams of engineers and technicians to manufacturers on a project-by-project basis. Essentially, you design solutions to manufacturing problems. You start your day by going through your voicemails and e-mails. You have some coffee and gather a notebook and head for a meeting with the other people on your team. An engineer has been working on a robotic solution for a major mail transport company. They want a machine that sorts envelopes of varying sizes. You are being called in to work on the electronics. Your team looks at the engineer's drawings, and you discuss possible problems and solutions. You break for lunch. After lunch, you begin assembling the wiring. The entire project will take months, but you have a good idea what you need already. The design will be based on robots already at work in the U.S. Post Office.

How to Break In

Take computer science and math classes while in high school. Join mechanics and robotics clubs, and take part in teams that build machines for scholastic competitions. Remember that you will benefit from having some kind of internship or related work experience to show prospective employers. A number of people in robotics now were retrained from dying fields in the 1980s; to stand out you can show you understand the latest robotics applications, such as robotic arms for surgeons. Use the job placement services of your college to your advantage. Keep in mind that additional technical and scientific skills, such as an understanding of chemistry, can translate to higher salaries in research and development. Techs in maintenance and repair tend to earn less.

Two-Year Training

You're going to want an associate's degree in an engineering specialty with more than adequate computer training. Many technical schools and community colleges offer robotics, although some call it electromechanics or applied science. Your training should encompass both the engineering and service of robotic systems. However, you need to develop an understanding of automated systems and basic engineering to be of most help to most employers. You should try to master as much computer-integrated manufacturing as you are able in the training phase. So take classes that bulk up your knowledge of computers and microprocessors. Dabble in electronics, hydraulics, and pneumatics. This is the kind of field in which you need a school that has all the "toys." Before you commit to a learning institution, see what its labs are like.

What to Look For in a School

Getting a good job will depend on how well the school taught you and how well connected your school really is. Before you start, ask these questions:

☞ Will I train on electrical equipment, such as motors and controllers?

☞ Is wiring a foundation of knowledge at the school?

☞ Will I learn about both the electronic and mechanical parts of the robots?

☞ Will I be taught to troubleshoot robotic problems, using related hardware and software?

☞ Do the professors have practical experience to share after working in the field?

☞ What internships are available?

☞ What is the school's track record for placing students in jobs?

The Future

Current market forces make robotics a smart career choice. To keep employees safe—and minimize health care costs—employers use robots to do the dirty and dangerous work, keeping their people out of production processes that could hurt them. In addition, robots often work at higher speeds and with greater efficiency than humans; the growing employment of machines is certain. This translates to job security for those who can manipulate robots. Meanwhile, related technology advances all the time, so the horizons of this relatively new field keep expanding. Being trained in robotics is forward thinking. Your personal rewards will include the chance to help build up the country's manufacturing might. You will probably continue your education on the job, taking classes in microelectronics advancements, for instance; but much of what you need to know you will learn while working, making things happen for your employer.

Did You Know?

Saturday morning cartoons are coming to life, just not the way we pictured them. Palo Alto Research Center is working on robots that morph, or mutate. They change shapes to adapt to each job. Household servant robots, working like Rosie in *The Jetsons*, will look one way to wash dishes and another to garden—probably in your lifetime.

Interview with a Professional:
Q&A
John Simpson

Automation specialist, Universal Technology,
Pittsburgh, Pennsylvania

Q: *How did you get started?*

A: Basically I like building things, monitoring things. As a kid, my hobby was building models. I was always pulling my bike apart. I knew I wanted to go into electronics. I attended a night school here in Pittsburgh and got a degree. They had ties with a place where I got a job upon graduation. I was doing field service work. Generally I'd report to the office. We'd receive robots. We'd have to make sure the robots looked good—were aesthetically appealing—and then we'd make sure they worked.

Q: *What's a typical day like?*

A: I'm working for Universal Technology, an automation company. Somebody comes in and wants to automate a process, and we figure out how to do that. Say it's [snack food company] Otis Spunkmeyer; they have a place in the Pittsburgh area. To make their muffins, they have to wash their pans. They wanted a robot to pick up a pan and put it on a conveyor and run it through the wash. On that project, I think there were three of us. We had a mechanical person do the layouts and the drawings. An electronics person worked on the electronics. And there was the programmer. There was also a project manager. In one day, we got the controller pretty much assembled. We came in with an empty box, and we mounted components—maybe got a start on the wiring.

Q: *What's your advice for those starting a career?*

A: Get into an electronics program or a technical school and have a good work ethic. You have to be on time every day. Be conscientious about your work. You want to do your best job all the time. There are some long days in the middle of a project. It's all about dedication.

Q: *What's the best part of your job?*

A: The thing I really like is that I'm not doing the same thing over and over. This doesn't get old. Every couple of months, there's a new project. The other thing is being able to take something from an idea and actually seeing it work. In my particular company, I'm more or less my own boss. I have freedom to get done what we need to do.

Job Seeking Tips

Follow these tips for finding employment in robotics. For help with writing résumés and handling interviews, turn to Appendix A.

✔ Evaluate your relative strengths and adjust your career search accordingly.

✔ Find relevant part-time employment before graduation.

✔ Join related trade and engineering groups.

✔ Get help from the career planning and placement office at your school.

Career Connections

For more information, contact the following organizations.

Accreditation Board for Engineering and Technology http://www.abet.org/

Automated Imaging Association http://www.machinevisiononline.org/

National Institute for Certification in Engineering Technologies http://www.nicet.org/

Robotics Industries Association http://www.robotics.org

International Society of Manufacturing Engineers http://www.sme.org

Associate's Degree Programs

Search online for schools that match your interests. Here are a few to get you started:

Community College of Allegheny County, Pittsburgh, Pennsylvania

Jefferson Community College, Steubenville, Ohio

Wake Technical Community College, Raleigh, North Carolina

Yuba Community College, Yuba City, California

Financial Aid

Here is a starting point for related scholarships. For additional information on financial aid, use Appendix B.

Computer Science Scholarship http://www.easyaid.com/computer

FIRST Scholarships http://www.usfirst.org/robotics/scholsh.htm

NASA Motivating Undergraduates in Science and Technology Scholarship http://www.hispanicfund.org

Xerox Technical Minority Scholarship http://www.xerox.com

Related Careers

Electric motor and switch assembler and repairer, electronics technician, field service representative, flexible manufacturing technician, and integrated manufacturing technician.

Chemical Technician

Vital Statistics

Salary: The median annual income for chemical technicians is about $38,000, according to 2006 data from the U.S. Bureau of Labor Statistics.

Employment: Forecasters say the greatest growth will be with firms that sell products, especially pharmaceuticals and custom items, to consumers. Companies being pushed to create more environmentally friendly products, such as plastics packagers, also need chemical technicians.The increase in jobs is expected to be slower than the average for all jobs through 2014, according to the Bureau of Labor Statistics.

Education: A solid chemistry and math background is essential. Earn at least an associate's degree in chemistry—or concentrate in chemistry while fulfilling requirements in engineering technology.

Work Environment: Work is often conducted in a laboratory. You will have a desk but may visit manufacturing areas. Keeping hazards to a minimum is an emphasis.

Ever try to read the label on your shampoo? How about the ingredients listed on a box of macaroni and cheese? When you break something into its chemical components, the list can be amazing. Most people who try reading the ingredients end up stumbling. The fact is, some people really do know one chemical from another and have an idea why each one is there.

The chemical engineering field attracts people who like to understand things at a very basic level. Chemical components can seem confusing to an outsider, but chemists love the simplicity of chemical building blocks and the somewhat predictable drama of their interactions. If that sounds at all like you—if you enjoy high school chemistry—consider taking the role of a chemical technician. There is plenty of reward in the field.

Chemical technicians develop, test, and manufacture chemicals and chemical products. The field encompasses a wide variety of goods, from plastics to paint, food to pharmaceuticals. Anything a chemical engineer works on, a technician works on as well. You could be making detergent. You could be working on fibers used for industrial products. Everything matters at this level of matter. The field combines chemistry and engineering; its practitioners bring their skills to the service of the manufacturing process.

Technicians work at all stages of manufacturing. Some are involved with research and development. Others are employed in design. Many work in

production. Still others are needed in quality control. Chemical technicians are in demand—now more than ever.

"Today, Ph.D. scientists are heavily involved in writing proposals, getting funding for research, and attending to other program requirements.
This means they spend more time outside of the lab," states Michael Cis-
neros, a chemical technician at Los Alamos National Laboratory, on the
Web site of the American Chemical Society. "As a result, they are handing
over to the technicians a lot more of the actual science than they have in
the past."

Technicians are trained to analyze the chemical composition of ingredients and products. One day, they might be looking for purity, or they might
be making sure a composition is stable. The design of the project is handled by the engineer in charge, but the technicians play an integral role.
They monitor the lab and record, analyze, and report data. Sometimes that
means preparing charts and diagrams. They are charged with making a vast
amount of data comprehensible.

Since World War II, the nature of the chemical technician's job has been
changing. Techs are now more than mere assistants. They exercise greater
responsibility and independence than ever.

If this line of work seems interesting to you, a free video about being a
"chem tech" is available from the American Chemical Society. Just go to
http://acswebcontent.acs.org/home.html.

"It's a very steady field," says Blake Aronson, who works in Technical
Education for the society and highly recommends the video. "Chemical
technology is not something that can be outsourced or shipped overseas."

On the Job

As a technician, you'll work as part of the engineering team. That team
varies depending on the industry in which you participate. Techs track
chemical compounds and their activity. They help improve the developmental process, offering insights they have earned from their inspections
and studies. Some even help develop new equipment used in the manufacture of chemicals or chemically based products. Without a doubt, the best
part of the job is its variety, say techs in research and manufacturing.

This is a hands-on position. You work with lab equipment: pipelines,
pumps, and valves. You use metal and glass tubes and tanks. Your firsthand
knowledge of the material is used to plan for material transfer. Moving
olives from one place to another is one thing. Moving a burning acid is
quite another! Your know-how is called upon to build and maintain the
equipment used for processing as well.

There are specialties within different industries, and the increased call
for techs in research and development is opening new levels of responsibility to chemical technicians. What's more, if you have organizational skills

and a team-building spirit, you can parlay your chemical engineering back-ground into some kind of management position. All of this translates into increased personal rewards.

Applied research technicians help with design and research. Other kinds of technicians test new construction materials or prepare tests for new chemicals in the field. Some specialize in fuel behavior. They test the flash point of fuels—the point at which fuels catch fire. They look for pour points—the coldest a fuel can be and still flow. They measure heat output.

With this job, you can find a way to apply yourself to the greater good of you, your family, your company, and the rest of us. We all benefit from the good work of chemical technicians. They make the modern world possible.

> ## "Few scientists [who are] acquainted with the chemistry of biological systems at the molecular level can avoid being inspired."
> —Donald Cram, Nobel Prize–winning chemist

 ## Keys to Success

To be successful in this field you should have or be good at

- analysis
- curiosity
- multitasking
- organization
- team spirit

Do You Have What It Takes?

Details! Details! You need to be a responsible kind of person who revels in details and can follow directions to the nth degree. Keen powers of observation are called for as well. Even the exactness of your color perception counts.

A chemical technician is good with his or her hands and connected to his or her brainpower. The job requires manual and mental dexterity. You must also be someone who can persevere when things go wrong. Patience is a virtue that's highly valued in the lab: Experiments are repeated to make sure they are right.

A Typical Day at Work

Let's say you work at a major food corporation in the United States. Although no day is like another day, you can bet that when you walk in the door, you will be spending approximately half your day on the floor and half your day upstairs, in your office. Different kinds of skills are called into play.

In food, chemical technicians perform many quality-control functions. The lines between these kinds of titles blur. During your time on the floor, you might be inspecting products coming down the line. Another day, you might be busy getting raw materials of the quality required.

The second half of the day, you take to your office and complete related paperwork. You fill out quality assurance reviews that have been developed internally. You call whom you need to call. You e-mail associates.

The very nature of the chemical tech's job can be rather secretive. You know how products come together, and you must keep what you know to yourself. Especially if you work in anything having to do with research and development, you will be told to keep what you know private.

How to Break In

The career placement office of your college can help you find jobs or hook you up with a recruiter. Try to fulfill a related internship while you are completing your degree. It shows your seriousness and prepares you for the real challenges of the profession. Join professional associations that can provide the contacts you need. Many also help with internships and summer jobs that add credibility to your résumé. Any industry or concern that involves chemistry hires technicians. Look for work at government agencies, in industries, and at universities. You might also find employment with a contractor who brings people like you in to work in various industries on a project-by-project basis.

Two-Year Training

In high school, take several years of science and math, along with whatever computer training that is available. Then apply yourself to at least a two-year technician program. Especially important are computer courses that teach you about word processing, spreadsheets, databases, and process control software—all needed to store and manipulate related data. Take chemistry courses that give you plenty of lab work. You'll need to master descriptive chemistry for organic and inorganic substances. You'll need to understand methods of analysis. Having a solid chemistry background will get you a job; employers hire the candidates requiring the least training on the job. Communications, industrial safety, math, and physics will round out your educational bill. Remember: There are hardly any industries that have no chemical testing whatsoever.

What to Look For in a School

When searching for the right school, ask these questions:

☞ Will the chemistry classes be extensive enough?

☞ Do the courses cover many areas of chemistry?

☞ Will the school meet my needs for computer classes?

☞ What is the career placement office's track record in placing graduates in internships and jobs?

☞ How much career-placement help does the school provide after graduation?

☞ What are the instructors' credentials?

The Future

You should think of the work you perform on the job as a continuing education and be prepared to take additional classes as needed. Many firms will help pay for further schooling. The field is alive with opportunity, especially in biotechnology, computers, energy fields, environmental concerns, materials science, and related quality control.

The fact that there is a deep-seated interest in making products that are friendlier to the environment will continue to spur new jobs in this field. The trend that takes research scientists out of the lab and into marketing will help open additional opportunities for chemical technicians within the laboratories.

Did You Know?

Louisiana and Texas usually pay the highest wages for chemical technicians. Why is that? The area is home to numerous chemical and petroleum companies along the Gulf Coast. Officials at offshore oil rigs and 24-hour refineries pay better than average.

Job Seeking Tips

These tips can help you land work as a chemical technician. Turn to Appendix A for general advice about résumés and interviewing:

✔ Decide which chemical field interests you and get related education.

✔ Enlist the help of the career placement professionals.

✔ Seek related work experience while in school.

✔ Read related materials from societies of chemists.

Interview with a Professional:
Q&A

Kelly Brownlee

Quality assurance lab technologist, Unilever
Foodsolutions, Belleville, Ontario

Q: *How did you get started in this line of work?*

A: I was a single mother and working as a food server at a local restaurant. I decided it was time to make a career change. I chose the chemical engineering technology program at Loyalist College in Belleville because of my love of science. After graduating from the program I applied to local companies.

Q: *What's a typical day like?*

A: Unilever Foodsolutions is a food manufacturing plant that produces drink crystals, nacho chips, liquid bouillon, bakery flakes, seasonings, and many varieties of dry soups, sauces, and gravies. On a typical day I evaluate samples of the different products that we are producing from all of the manufacturing lines in the plant. There are a range of tests and analyses that I perform, depending on the type of product produced. Many of the products produced require simple sensory evaluations for color, flavor, and appearance. Other products require additional analytical testing such as pH, moisture analysis, sieve analysis, viscosity, specific gravity and percentage salt, to name a few. I am also required to perform audits of the processing plant and review, update, and implement standard operating and quality procedures to help ensure we are producing top quality products.

Q: *What's your advice for those starting a career?*

A: Don't limit yourself to jobs in a chemical laboratory. A diploma in chemical engineering technology can apply to a wide variety of lab positions. Don't be afraid to apply for positions in labs that aren't necessarily chemical in nature. Challenge yourself—you may be surprised at what you're able to accomplish.

Q: *What's the best part of your job?*

A: I enjoy the variety in my job. Every day is different and presents its own set of challenges. I like that my job encompasses both analytical testing and computer and desk work. I am challenged every day to stay sharp and keep my mind focused to ensure that my plant is producing top quality food products.

Career Connections

For more information, contact the following organizations.

American Association for Clinical Chemistry http://www.aacc.org

American Chemical Society http://www.acs.org

American Chemistry Council http://www.americanchemistry.org

American Institute of Chemical Engineers http://www.aiche.org

Associate's Degree Programs

Search online for schools that match your interests. Here are a few to get you started:

Miami University Middletown, Middletown, Montana

Northern New Mexico College, Española, New Mexico

Northwest College, Powell, Wyoming

St. Paul College, St. Paul, Minnesota

Financial Aid

This list of scholarships relates to chemists. Check Appendix B for more financial aid tips.

American Chemical Society Scholarships http://www.cnetweb.org/american_chemical_society_scholarships.htm

DuPont Challenge Science Essay Competition http://www.qlcomm.com/dupont/

RockOn! Scholarships http://www.rock-on.ca/scholarship.htm

Related Careers

Energy technician, environmental engineering technician, formulation technician, lab technician, lab tester, research associate, quality control technician, and science technician.

Laser Technician

Salary: The average annual income for laser technicians in all their variety of fields is about $43,000, according to 2006 data from the U.S. Bureau of Labor Statistics.

Employment: The opportunities for laser technicians are expanding as fast as the average for all jobs through 2014—according to the Bureau of Labor Statistics—as laser applications multiply, with growth potential especially good in rapidly advancing areas of technology, such as fiber optics.

Education: Employment prospects are strong with a two-year degree in a good laser, electro-optics, or photonics technology program.

Work Environment: Laser technicians will usually work inside, in a clean, temperature-controlled space.

Lasers were once a matter of science fiction. Beams of light would shine in bold relief in comic-book tales about advanced worlds. High beams served as both weapons and instruments of healing in sci-fi books and films. Just talking about lasers, you can almost hear the *swoosh* of light sabers from a *Star Wars* movie.

The technology has long since come down to Earth. We even have laser toys these days; perhaps you, too, can recall playing laser tag with a plastic "power pack." Lasers are part of our everyday world, and photonics technology has improved so much more than our sources of amusement. Controlled light sources accomplish certain tasks faster and more precisely than any tools that have come before.

"Photonics is the general term encompassing all fields or industries involving the use of light more technically referred to as photons," says Al Ducharme, a professor of photonics at the University of Central Florida, Orlando, Florida. "Photonics technology is used in almost every product we use today. A cell phone includes a liquid crystal screen and several light-emitting diodes, both photonic devices. There are literally thousands of companies that employ engineers who specialize in photonics technology. This is because every day new products are brought to market that utilize photonics in some way."

When you picture lasers, you might think first of the laser light presentations at major city celebrations and at big concerts. Lasers can be incredibly pretty, like a controlled fireworks display; but it is the practical, even life-saving aspects of laser applications that are probably most beautiful.

The power of light has been harnessed to perform important medical operations in doctors' offices and research labs—creating astounding advances and cutting healing times. Certainly, there are cosmetic applications, such as laser hair and tattoo removal, but lasers are used to fix nonfunctioning arteries, remove cataracts, and save lives.

Lasers are instrumental in manufacturing processes as well. By their very nature, lasers are wonderfully precise tools. They can be used to scan and replicate expensive *templates*, which are the patterns for almost any design these days, and they take highly accurate measurements. This ability has many uses: Lasers check the contours of automobile seats and fit them with seatbelts. Photonics are used in all aspects of airplane manufacture. After those planes are air worthy, safety personnel use infrared cameras to inspect every inch of these planes, searching for cracks and abnormalities and keeping passengers safe. Lasers have sped up and improved this entire inspection process.

"In today's job world, photonics ranks as one of the hottest fields," says Ducharme. "There are educational options available for two-year, four-year, and graduate school to train you for the photonics field."

On the Job

Laser technicians take advantage of this relatively new field by learning to repair, install, operate, and test laser equipment. They guarantee themselves gainful employment by earning the training and certification needed.

These engineering techs work with either solid-state laser systems or those of a gas type. The first kind is compact, with miniature devices that are used on computer and telephone systems. The second is large and costly, and is used in manufacturing, medical, and robotics systems.

As an engineering tech, you might analyze the computer readouts of a laser that scans circuits. Or you might be involved with lasers employed in robotics or another aspect of manufacturing. Lasers do cutting, heating, and welding. They harden materials. They engrave items.

Techs are assigned to different stages of production. Some people might be welding metals with lasers. Others drill, cut, and grind materials. Some manipulate and measure electronics. Others might be repairing laser equipment itself. Others will be building lasers—from the crystal rods inside to the flash tubes and mirrors outside.

Still others work with optical fibers. In most kinds of laser technology that you might be hired to perform, you would also program the lasers' computers. You would make reports.

Whether your work is relatively stationary or you regularly visit laboratories and production sites as well will depend on the assignment. Strict safety measures will be enforced, such as the use of safety goggles.

Keys to Success

To be successful in this field you should have

- manual dexterity
- math aptitude
- problem-solving skills
- science aptitude
- self-direction

Do You Have What It Takes?

You should be someone who likes to manipulate devices—a gadget person. You should be comfortable being in charge of instruments and you should have a sense for the logical order of things. A good laser technician is also coordinated. Need it be said that highly intense beams of light can be dangerous in the wrong hands? Since technicians may use highly expensive pieces of equipment, mistakes can be costly. You need to be someone responsible who can work with patience and perform in a careful and efficient manner. Laser techs need a high degree of mechanical aptitude. You should also be drawn to technical and scientific topics.

A Typical Day at Work

With so many applications for this technology, it's hard to describe a typical day at work. If you live in Detroit, Michigan, you might operate a welding laser on an auto assembly line. In Portland, Oregon, you might operate a scanner for circuits. In New York City, you might be operating a cutter, making patterns through multiple layers of cloth for the garment industry. Perhaps you live in Los Angeles. If so, you might work at a company that provides subtitles in the manufacture of films. As a laser technician, you would run the machine that etches subtitles onto what's called the "emulsion" layer of film. In all these jobs, your day might involve your making a safety check of the machinery and dealing with any irregularities, using a troubleshooting guide, your knowledge, and the know-how of the rest of your team. You are responsible for day-to-day operations and for perfecting your company's product. You are relied upon for your technical expertise.

How to Break In

In high school, be sure to take computer sciences courses. Take math and physics too. If the school teaches electronics and machine shop, go for it. Find a good program in a vocational or tech school to build on your solid base.

Check related associations for certifications that might help you be more employable. The Laser Institute of America, for instance, offers certification as a laser safety officer. Then, during your two-year program, try to secure related work. Seek help from your career placement center to find employment after graduation.

To stand out, be someone who can write a clear, well-organized report. Be sure to take the classes that build on your English fundamentals, and take them seriously.

"Another benefit of laser scanning is that scanning provides actual x, y, and z coordinates. . . . Manufacturing can see exactly how much [a process] is off."
—Jud Kittel, senior development engineer, Lear Corporation

Two-Year Training

The training you get should includes a ton of laboratory work. Becoming adept with lasers requires hands-on training. You'll also extend the knowledge base you gathered in high school in math, physics, computers, electronics, and drafting.

The best programs will offer courses in manufacturing systems and processes, including design. You should be well versed in computer skills, interactive media, and network systems. Consider some basic business courses as well, with classes such as global economics. You'll want to be prepared to follow your career into management. This also means you should pay attention to your writing and speaking skills. You never know what you will be called upon to do.

As your training nears an end, you will be introduced to the many aspects of lasers: circuits, electro-optics, microcomputers, microwaves, vacuums, and more.

What to Look For in a School

When searching for the right school, ask these questions:

☞ Is this school closely connected with employers in the area and elsewhere?

☞ What is the school's job placement rate?

☞ How helpful is the career planning office?

☞ Will there be much lab work?

☞ Will the science behind the practical operations be covered?

☞ What are the instructors' credentials?

The Future

Lasers have been described as "a solution seeking problems," according to the federal government's Solutions for Advanced Manufacturing Web site. This field is relatively new, by many measures, and the future applications seem limitless.

As with most highly technical jobs, you should expect to continue your training as the years progress, in order to stay current with new developments. The area of fiber optics is especially promising, as optical fiber replaces wire cables. Other areas of growth include construction, entertainment, medicine, and the military. "From our standpoint, a career in optics is great," says Eric Van Stryland, dean of the College of Optics and Photonics at the University of Central Florida. "Our students get excellent job offers, good jobs in industry performing research and engineering, project engineering, etc. And more [technicians] are needed."

Did You Know?

Talk about a power pack. The Nova laser, at the Lawrence Livermore National Laboratory in California, is three stories tall. Built to reproduce conditions at the center of the sun, it can target something the size of a grain of sand with 100 trillion watts of energy.

Job Seeking Tips

Here are tips specific to photonics. For additional advice related to résumés and job interviews, check Appendix A.

✔ Let the career counselors at your school hook you up with job possibilities.

✔ Ask instructors to make networking introductions.

✔ Line up related summer work well before you graduate.

✔ Search the Internet for related research projects.

✔ Join related associations and volunteer at their conferences.

Interview with a Professional:
Q&A
Cody Hulse
Depot engineer/laser tech repair, Lumenis, Inc.,
Salt Lake City, Utah

Q: *How did you get started in this line of work?*

A: I was first introduced to lasers as a career in high school. The counselors at school set up tours for us at [a technology college]. They gave us information on the different programs we could see there, and we were told to pick three to visit on tour day. I picked lasers because it sounded like fun stuff out of the movies. When we got there we had a small light show set up using an argon laser and mirrors. They had several other experiments on display. They made it seem even more interesting than I had thought. No light sabers, but more scientific thinking! That coupled with the fact that with only two years of school, I could make a larger salary than many of my friends who spent four-plus years made the decision fairly easy for me.

Q: *What's a typical day like?*

A: I am working for a medical laser company, where I repair surgical, ophthalmic, and aesthetic lasers. They are used by everyone from veterinarians treating animals to medical doctors helping people with cataracts. I receive the laser into our repair facility in Salt Lake City. We first evaluate the problems, troubleshoot, and repair any issues and test it to ensure that it will continue to work without any issues for the doctors using them.

Q: *What's your advice for those starting a career?*

A: Focus on your troubleshooting and problem-solving skills. No matter where you go, if you have those skills you will be one of the top people there. This really goes for any field you go into. I was the guy in class who always asked, "When are we ever going to use this?" Well, I can honestly say that I use a lot of the math I complained about, and what I don't use, I know, leads me to better problem-solving skills.

Q: *What's the best part of your job?*

A: I enjoy the freedom that the job allows me to have. I am able to work on different laser systems and am able to constantly solve new problems. That makes it exciting to me. It also gives me the freedom to spend more time doing the things I like in my off time.

Career Connections

For more information, contact the following organizations.

Association for Manufacturing Technology http://www.photonics.com

Center for Laser Aided Manufacturing http://engr.smu.edu/clam/

Institute of Electrical and Electronics Engineers http://www.ieee.org/leos

International Society of Optical Engineering http://www.spie.org

Laser Institute of America http://www.laserinstitute.org/

Solutions for Advanced Manufacturing http://strategis.ic.gc.ca/epic/internet/insam-sfp.nsf/en/Home

Associate's Degree Programs

Search online for schools that match your interests. Here are a few to get you started:

Camden County College, Blackwood, New Jersey

Idaho State University, Pocatello, Idaho

Kaua'i Community College, Lihue, Hawaii

Merced College, Los Banos, California

Financial Aid

Several related scholarships follow. Look in Appendix B for more financial advice.

Great Lakes Photonic Scholarship http://www.lci.kent.edu

International Society for Optical Engineering http://www.spie.org/app/education/index.cfm

NASA Motivating Student Undergraduates in Science and Technology http://www.nasa.gov/centers/marshall/education/index.html

Xerox Technical Minority Scholarship http://www.xerox.com/

Related Careers

Fiber optics technician, laser consultant, laser field technician, laser machine operator, laser salesperson, medical laser technician, technical writer, and telecommunications technician.

Microelectronics Technician

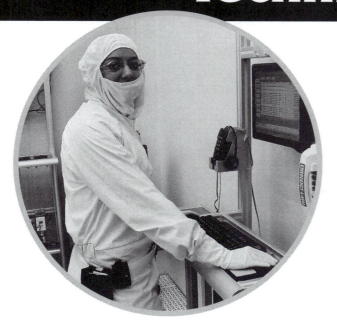

Vital Statistics

Salary: Microelectronics technicians earn a median annual income of about $42,000, according to 2006 data from the U.S. Bureau of Labor Statistics.

Employment: Rising efficiency and the globalization of the industry spell a decline in electronics jobs through 2014, according to the Bureau of Labor Statistics. Some growth is forecast in the area of biomedical and measuring intruments.

Education: Concentrate on English, math, and physics in high school. Earn a technological degree from a good two-year institution.

Work Environment: You will work inside, often in a development laboratory, where your help is needed most. These sites are very clean, given the nature of the product.

Electronics are essential to modern life. The practical science of manipulating electricity makes TVs, radar, and microwaves possible. Employees skilled in electronics and microelectronics corral and divert electrical energy to a universe of practical uses, not the least of which is computer networking.

Jesse Allen is a workforce development manager for Intel Corporation in Hillsboro, Oregon. From where he sits, job prospects in microelectronics look very good. "As long as there are computers and we're producing computer chips, I see there's going to be a need for technicians," he says.

Intel is a leader in the manufacturing of computer, networking, and communications products. The company is also the world's largest computer chip maker; hence, the "Intel Inside" brand you find on so many products.

When Intel needed more microelectronics technicians in Oregon to support its manufacturing programs there, the company partnered with area schools to provide training for students. Local colleges offered two-year degrees in the basic principles and concepts of related manufacturing technology; Intel started an internal program of training for its operators. "From there it evolved into microelectronics," says Allen.

Allen says the work is essential and can be exciting. You "get to see the latest and greatest [computer products] before the public sees them," he says. It's amazing when you think of it: Tiny computer chips conduct almost all the information that makes our computerized economy run.

Chips are teeny pieces, typically one-quarter inch wide, of material on which an integrated circuit is embedded. The semiconducting material used is usually silicon; hence the nickname "Silicon Valley" for the area in California where so many of the major computer concerns are based. Computers, in essence, are many chips on electronic boards.

Microelectronics is all about *integrated circuits*, the tiny enablers that allow engineers to build electronic devices in miniature. These amazingly minuscule integrated circuits started out as state secrets; they were originally developed for the military and the space programs. These days, microchips power and guide devices that have touched all corners of our everyday world.

These thin strips of semiconducting material hold layers of information along complex circuits. They contain vast amounts of data and can be used in all kinds of applications. There are the "ah, gee" kind of uses: People are planting them in their pets, in case the family dog gets away and can't find its way home. However, other kinds of implementations are simply awesome in power and scope: Chips are used in communications equipment and industrial controls. They guide both spaceships and the lifesaving power equipment used on the operating table.

On the Job

Pass the chips! As a microelectronics technician, you deal with chips in a hands-on and practical way. Some technicians design and build them. Others test and repair them. You work as a team with electronics engineers, often getting products ready for manufacturing.

You might be given a design listing the microelectronic components and their layout. A number of kinds of chips might be involved in a design. You build and then test your work, seeing how long the item will last in nonstop operation.

Being a microelectronics technician is all about being a smooth operator. You understand related processing, testing, and assembly equipment. You internalize related procedures. You read needed specifications.

You clean, coat, and bake chips. You layer material. It almost sounds like being a baker, but you're working with material that eats information, rather than creating something that's presented to take the edge off human hunger. You implant chemicals at select points on the wafers to change the course of the electrical path. You assemble, mount, bond, and package the devices. This is exacting and important work.

Knowing how to make and manipulate electrical energy is a skill worth having, an aptitude that you can sell for a long time to come. These tiny instruments are complex electronic devices that we all rely upon to a high degree yet few of us understand fully. Knowing their worlds within our world can help you land and keep satisfying employment that helps everyone live a full and modern life. Just be ready to adapt as your career moves along! In the quest to improve products, there is constant change.

Keys to Success

To be successful in this field, you should possess
- communications skills
- independent work habits
- intellectual curiosity
- problem solving skills
- technical understanding
- the ability to work well in a team

Do You Have What It Takes?

To thrive in this line of work, you should enjoy technical and scientific subjects. You need to have a blend of skill sets. On one hand, you should be able to think clearly and logically and follow directions. On the other, you need a steady hand and a certain amount of manual skill. Precision counts on this job. You should also be a good communicator. You will be explaining the specifications of computer components, reporting on your evaluations, and in some cases, training others to build these tiny masterpieces.

A Typical Day at Work

The design engineer who is currently leading your team provided a schematic drawing for a computer component. You and the rest of the technicians followed the layout perfectly, but the component failed in testing yesterday. It now becomes your job to troubleshoot. You interpret and evaluate the processing data. You must pinpoint the problem so the team can replace the failed section or parts. That afternoon, you address the problem with the engineer. You spend the rest of the day making the replacement. Later, you will test the component again, creating successful test results you can report to senior staff. Everything you are learning as you decipher this problem will become part of any technical writing explaining the component's design. The specifications you arrive at together will be used in the manufacture of the component.

How to Break In

You absolutely need education and training for at least an associate's degree in microelectronics technology to enter this field with odds stacked in your favor. Take computer science, industrial arts, math, and physics in high school. Make sure you do not allow your communications skills to lag behind. Your post–high school training should continue in these subjects. Look for related work as early as possible, while in school. Perhaps there is something in electronics repair available. You can learn a lot on a job like that. Also consider earning additional certifications through associations such as the International Society of Certified Electronics Technicians. Such certifications may help you be a more desirable employee and set you apart as someone worth promoting.

Two-Year Training

Many schools that offer good training in the field are located in areas of the country where there is a crushing need for microelectronics technicians. Your coursework will include chemistry, math, physics, and electronic engineering. You will be given a foundation in the basics before moving on to the nitty-gritty of semiconductor manufacturing, equipment operation, and vacuum and plasma technology. You will divide your time between labs and classrooms. A good school will require writing courses. There will probably be coursework related to business speech and communication. These are the so-called soft skills that can help you get ahead no matter where you land after graduation. All these classes will prepare you for the on-the-job training that is part of this work. Each industry has its own ways of teaching its nuances and welcoming you into the fold.

What to Look For in a School

When searching for the right school, ask these questions:

☞ How up-to-date are the labs?

☞ What related working background do the instructors have?

☞ Does the school offer on-the-job training programs?

☞ What kinds of job placement services are there?

☞ Does the school have ties with major manufacturers?

☞ Where do graduates end up five years down the line?

The Future

In the decade leading to 2014, output in microelectronics is expected to increase more rapidly than any other business, according to the U.S. Department of Labor. That will not equal an overall increase in jobs, however, so be wary. Older workers will have to be replaced and new technologies introduced, so jobs will become available, especially in navigational, measuring, and electromedical manufacturing. However, the greatest opportunities will be in research and development. Your knowledge can be used to simplify processes for your employer, improving everything from product assembly to the supervising of other personnel. Some techs will be involved in the creation of prototypes—things not seen before. Just keep in mind that you must continue your training as you work. Advances in the field are continuous and rapid. You do not want to be left behind!

Interview with a Professional:
Q&A

Licia Bilyeu

Microelectronics technician at Intel Corporation,
Hillsboro, Oregon

Q: *How did you get started in this line of work?*

A: In high school I tried to take as many computer-oriented classes as possible because I realized that no matter what career path I chose I was going to be using computers in some way or another. I heard about the career opportunities as a microelectronics technician at my local community college through an open house hosted by Intel Corporation.

Q: *What's a typical day like?*

A: We work in a "clean room" environment that is a thousand times cleaner than a hospital operating room. Each silicon wafer has approximately 550 microprocessors on it, and the wafers are processed in groups of 25 at a time. Each 25-wafer lot goes through hundreds of steps on different process equipment that builds the transistors and connections that make up the microprocessor. Each microprocessor is about the size of a human thumbnail and has approximately over 42 million transistors. The transistors are like switches. They open or close, letting electrical current through or preventing it from going through. Every different area of the fab [fabrication facility] has designated teams of technicians who are responsible for running wafers through their areas. A microelectronics technician's job is about 80 percent team effort and 20 percent individual effort.

Q: *What's your advice for those starting a career?*

A: If you enjoy hands-on technical work and troubleshooting, a career in microelectronics would definitely be an excellent career choice. My advice would be to take over and above the required math and science classes that your school offers. Physics and chemistry are important science classes to take, and algebra, trigonometry, discrete math, and probability and statistics are math classes that will help prepare you for this career.

Q: *What's the best part of your job?*

A: The best thing about my job is definitely the people I work with. I enjoy working in a team environment with other technicians, engineers, and managers. I've met so many wonderful, highly intelligent people who are all working toward a common goal: developing the best microprocessors available on the market today.

Did You Know?

Being satisfied with how things are is not always good. Intel's cofounder Gordon Moore built the company with this guiding principle: The number of transistors on a microprocessor should double every 18 months to two years. This mandate for improvement has become standard throughout the industry.

Job Seeking Tips

Follow these tips for finding work as a microelectronics technician. Turn to Appendix A for general help with résumés and interview techniques.

✔ Seek related employment and internships before graduation.

✔ Use the resources of the career placement department.

✔ Follow the trade magazines and Web sites such as that of the American Electronics Association at http://www.aeanet.org/.

✔ Ask instructors for contacts, and join professional organizations.

> **"Computer science is the only discipline in which we view adding a new wing to a building as being maintenance."**
> —Jim Horning, Stanford University computer science instructor

Career Connections

For more information, contact the following organizations.

American Electronics Association http://www.aeanet.org

Association of Super-Advanced Electronics Technologies http://www.aset.org/

Electronics Industry Alliance http://www.eia.org

International Society of Certified Electronics Technicians http://www.iscet.org

Surface Mount Technology Association http://www.smta.org

Associate's Degree Programs

Search online for schools that match your interests. Here are a few to get you started:

Clackamas Community College, Oregon City, Oregon

Niagra College, Niagra-on-the-Lake, Ontario

Penn State McKeesport, McKeesport, Pennsylvania

Valencia Community College, Orlando, Florida

Financial Aid

Several related scholarships follow. For more on financial aid for two-year students, look in Appendix B.

International Communications Industries Foundation
http://www.infocomm.org/foundation/

National Security Agency Cooperative Education Program
http://www.nsa.gov/careers/students.cfm

Penn State McKeesport Scholarships http://www.mk.psu.edu/
Academics/scholarships.htm

Reuben Trane Scholarship http://www.ashrae.org/students/page/704

Related Careers

Assembler and fabricator, computer hardware engineer, computer software engineer, database administrator, electronic engineering technician, engineering technician, inspector, and semiconductor processor.

Plastics Technician

Vital Statistics

Salary: Depending on duration of work, skill, and job specifics such as company size and union status, plastics technicians earn from an annualized $24,000 operating casting machines to $44,000 as model makers, according to 2006 data from the U.S. Bureau of Labor Statistics.

Employment: Employment of machinists, including plastics technicians, is expected to decrease through 2014 as automation and foreign competition reduce hiring needs domestically according to the Bureau of Labor Statistics. Plastics machinists will be in greater demand than those who work with metal.

Education: Earn at least an associate's degree in plastics engineering. Get a solid background in computer numerical control and related technologies to advance in this career.

Work Environment: Some technicians work in the controlled environment of a lab. Others report to plants or small shops.

These days, plastics take us from birth to the grave. Plastic diapers, toys, dishes, containers, calculator covers, MP3s, furniture, keyboards: The list is endless.

Name a sport. In baseball, there is plastic on helmets, cleats, catchers' gear—even the bases. In cycling, bikers use mountain and road bikes with key plastic parts. Tires are reinforced with plastic. Those trim spandex outfits are a flexible plastic material.

As a plastics technician, you can only begin to imagine what might happen over the course of your career. China, for instance, has rapidly developed into the world's leading importer of engineering plastics, used mainly to make Chinese autos, electronics, and electrical appliances. The plastics field might translate into international opportunities for you.

Future plastics applications promise to be amazing. Right now, the U.S. government, a partnership of American automakers, Argonnne National Laboratory, and the American Plastics Council are working to create a futuristic car that can be recycled. Imagine that.

"Plastics are the future," says Bonnie Knopf, owner of Intrepid Plastics Manufacturing, in Michigan. "There are so many types, from the bottom of your shoe to the surgical components in the medical industry. It is amazing to be involved in plastics development, whether it is in the design, tooling, processing, or testing of materials." The plastics industry is diverse in other ways as well. There is injection molding for making primarily solid parts, extrusion (a shaping process) for pipes and window blinds, blow molding for bottles, thermo molding for sheet products, and many others.

Many plastics techs are attracted to the futuristic aspects of the material. They work in research and development, helping to create new plastics or to make improvements to the plastics already known. Knowledge of plastics is needed for countless common manufacturing applications too. If the wrong material is used during the production of an outdoor product, such as the lounge chair on a patio, the UV rays from the sun could discolor it; but you can use UV stabilizers to make the color last for years. Molds are tricky, and each one is a new puzzle. You need to monitor the raw goods that are used. You need to inspect the end products.

Each day, each job, is another story. "The process varies depending on indoor and outdoor temperatures, the moisture in the material, the speed at which the plastic is injected into the mold, and even how it cools," says Knopf.

Some techs place plastics on top of products—a special skill brought to bear when creating surfboards. Others find their calling as fabricators, who use machine-shop skills in the plastics area. Others find their communication skills are valued in related sales and service. After all, buying plastic is a science. If you can explain things well and listen closely, you might find you're needed to help customers select the right plastic and molds for their needs and budget. No matter which area of the plastics industry you choose, you will have input that, in its own way, affects the future.

On the Job

You go into the shop knowing that your schedule will be based on the purchase or work orders the company has received. If you work for a specific manufacturer, say, a toy company, your days might resemble one another for longer periods of time, as specific toys, such as a kind of kiddie car, are developed and become popular. If you work for a plastics group that provides parts to larger manufacturers, the days vary by the kind of jobs on the docket.

Let's say you work in a shop in an area in which the automotive industry is big. You are likely needed for automotive projects, so new jobs will often resemble other jobs but with interesting differences. In each case, you must create molds for the plastics parts. Your team starts by making prototypes designed on a computer. You enter specifications into the programming and study the cutting sequence the computer recommends. With some trial and error, you find the winning mold and decide how the company can best manufacture it. Along with the mold, you often must come up with new tools and dies. Talk about working from scratch!

Precision measuring instruments are at the die makers' disposal; but what they most need is a good sense for a plastic's hardness and heat tolerance, and a working base of math and blueprint skills. Throughout the process, they must stay attuned to the accuracy of the tools. This isn't cooking: An extra pinch could mean failure. They then fit the part, using files and grinders. Afterward, it's time to test their outcome: How does it work, after all that effort?

Keys to Success

To be successful as a plastics technician, you should possess

- creativity
- manual dexterity
- math and spatial skills
- organization skills
- problem solving skills

Do You Have What It Takes?

This is a job that requires manual dexterity, precision, and physical effort. If you read between the lines, you realize that the work also calls for a good deal of patience. You can't rush through inventive, detailed, manual employment like this. You should also have keen listening skills and follow-through. Those who take satisfaction from solving problems will enjoy the work. A good sense of organization provides a strong base for success. Be aware that color blindness can hold you back; but strong communications skills will help you advance.

A Typical Day at Work

Let's say you work in lab, and it is your job to help conduct tests and monitor results. You are usually looking for a plastic's properties, as outlined by the research engineer who usually heads your team. At the end of the process, you must write your part of the report. Today you set up a test that will make certain the plastic parts of a waffle maker are right. Your lab has been hired by a major appliance maker for whom the waffle maker is a new product. The appliance company has a signature green plastic used on its top-line goods, and the waffle maker will be offered in that line even though it would be easier to make the item all metal. You gather your gauges. You take nothing for granted. The item could be changed since its manufacture. The heating apparatus inside the machine could alter the plastic's shape and color during the testing process. You heat the machine. As the time passes, you send e-mails to your supervisor regarding upcoming work for another manufacturer. So far, so good. You break for lunch. All that time thinking about waffles made you hungry.

How to Break In

To take advantage of the wide variety of work available in the plastics field, take math and the laboratory sciences, including chemistry and physics, while in high school. Industrial arts and English will help as well. Go to vocational camps if possible. Then complete a well-rounded two-year plastics program at a good two-year school and try to gain on-the-job experience while you do. Join professional groups such as the Society of Plastics Engineers. Strive to find the right job for yourself through career placement at your school, your instructors, who probably have contacts, and your own efforts through professional societies.

> ## "My stockbroker asked me something important today: paper or plastic?"
> —Jay Leno, comedian

Two-Year Training

Plastics training is often offered at technical schools as part of the mechanical or chemical technicians programs. Sometimes it is referred to as "plastics process." No matter how your school labels the related training program, your classes should include plenty of lab work. You should be given a good background in math, chemistry, drawing, and safety principles. You should be encouraged to master measurement: bulk, fluid, linear, temperature, and power and force. Your school should provide training that covers the basics of plastics and the principles of electricity. You'll learn about plastics molding and fabrication. There should be instruction in thermoplastics, reinforced plastics, synthetics, foams, and testing procedures. Some robotics should be involved. After completing the program, you should be able to meet the related standards put forward by the U.S. Department of Labor's Bureau of Apprenticeship and Training and earn their industry-recognized certification.

What to Look For in a School

When searching for the right school, ask these questions:

☞ Does the program cover standards mandated by the Bureau of Apprenticeship and Training?

☞ Is there a work-study program?

☞ Will I learn plastic processes, electrical concepts, and statistical process control?

☞ Will I learn injection molding, principles of heat transfer, and safety and testing?

☞ What is the job placement rate?

☞ Do the instructors have recent practical experience in the field?

The Future

Scientists all over the world are testing new plastics and applications in the search for new properties and uses. Polymeric materials promise to yield materials that resist scratches and friction and survive high heat and impacts—recyclable goods that will have many lives and help many lives.

Your chances for advancement in the field grow as you take on challenges. Take advantage of on-site training programs at work, such as those that develop managerial skills. Learn languages if you hope to work in other countries, and stay in tune with advances and new applications. Employment opportunities are expected to be excellent, according to the most recent *Occupational Outlook Handbook* data (2004). The number of jobs is not expected to grow, because computers are making it easier for one person to do more work. But fewer people are in related training right now, so that means you have an opportunity to step right in.

Did You Know?

Plastics can be traced back to 1869, when a billiards company offered $10,000—a hunk of change at the time—to come up with a ball not made of ivory. (The elephant tusks in use were becoming rare and costly.) That's when John Wesley Hyatt came up with an early plastic he called celluloid.

Job Seeking Tips

Follow these tips, relevant to the plastics industry, and turn to Appendix A for help with writing your résumé and interview techniques.

✔ Find related employment while taking classes.

✔ Ask your instructors for tips on finding jobs.

✔ Get help from your school's career placement office.

✔ Join professional groups that meet in your area.

Interview with a Professional:
Q&A
Bonnie Knopf
Custom molder, Intrepid Plastics Manufacturing,
Comstock Park, Michigan

Q: *How did you get started in this line of work?*

A: I started into the plastics program following a recommendation from my [college] adviser. I [completed] an internship with Intrepid Plastics Manufacturing. This turned out to be a great experience, as I was able to see many different aspects of the industry. The opportunity to see quality control at work [was] an excellent one to show the importance of process and product control in industry.

Q: *What's a typical day like?*

A: A typical day? I don't think there is such a thing for a custom molder. Activities range from changing tools and running parts to collecting quality control data and creating charts. There is a constant variety to look forward to and a new challenge each day.

Q: *What's your advice for those starting a career?*

A: Do the best you can in school; it has a bigger impact on your future than you might expect. Also, if you need to complete an internship, try to find a company that will allow you to experience several different areas of the industry that you're working in. Also, make your résumé and cover letter as close to perfect as possible . . . in terms of grammar and spelling.

Q: *What's the best part of your job?*

A: The single best part about being in plastics is the variety. There is a never-ending list of places where plastics are used. There are so many different ways to experience [the field] other than automotive. The appeal here is that if you happen to get bored with one area, there's always another to get involved in. There are several major ways that plastic can be processed and a host of other minor ways to turn it into a part. Simply put, there's no way to completely exhaust the different opportunities available in the plastics industry.

Career Connections

For more information, contact the following organizations.

American Plastics Council http://www.plastics.org

National Tooling and Machining Association http://www.ntma.org

Precision Machine Products Association http://www.pmpa.org

Society of Plastics Engineers http://www.4spe.org/

Society of Plastics Industry http://www.socplas.org

Associate's Degree Programs

Search online for schools that match your interests. Here are a few to get you started:

Community College of Rhode Island, Warwick, Rhode Island

Edison State Community College, Piqua, Ohio

Ferris State University, Big Rapids, Michigan

Wake Technical Community College, Raleigh, North Carolina

Financial Aid

Related scholarships include those listed below. Look in Appendix B for additional tips on financial aid.

Boeing Technology Scholarship http://www.boeing.com/educationrelations/scholarships/

Plastic Molders Scholarship Foundation http://www.plasticmolders.org/scholarship/index.htm

Plastics Institute of America www.eng.uml.edu/Dept/PIA/public_html

Society of Plastics Engineers http://www.4spe.org

Related Careers

Aircraft, appliance, computer, and electronics manufacturer; assembler, fabricator; quality control personnel; laboratory manager; machine setter, operator, or tender; machinist; product designer; production manager; and purchasing agent.

Appendix A
Tools for Career Success

When 20-year-old Justin Schulman started job-hunting for a position as a fitness trainer—his first step toward managing a fitness facility—he didn't mess around. "I immediately opened the Yellow Pages and started calling every number listed under health and fitness, inquiring about available positions," he recalls. Schulman's energy and enterprise paid off: He wound up with interviews that led to several offers of part-time work.

Schulman's experience highlights an essential lesson for jobseekers: There are plenty of opportunities out there, but jobs won't come to you—especially the career-oriented, well-paying ones that that you'll want to stick with over time. You've got to seek them out.

Uncover Your Interests

Whether you're in high school or bringing home a full-time paycheck, the first step toward landing your ideal job is assessing your interests. You need to figure out what makes you tick. After all, there is a far greater chance that you'll enjoy and succeed in a career that taps into your passions, inclinations, and natural abilities. That's what happened with career-changer Scott Rolfe. He was already 26 when he realized he no longer wanted to work in the food industry. "I'm an avid outdoorsman," Rolfe says, "and I have an appreciation for natural resources that many people take for granted." Rolfe turned his passions into his ideal job as a forest technician.

If you have a general idea of what your interests are, you're far ahead of the game. You may know that you're cut out for a health care career, for instance, or one in business. You can use a specific volume of *Top Careers in Two Years* to discover what position to target. If you are unsure of your direction, check out the whole range of volumes to see the scope of jobs available. Ask yourself, what job or jobs would I most like to do if I *already* had the training and skills? Then remind yourself that this is what your two-year training will accomplish.

You can also use interest inventories and skills-assessment programs to further pinpoint your ideal career. Your school or public librarian or guidance counselor should be able to help you locate such assessments. Web sites such as America's Career InfoNet (http://www.acinet.org) and JobWeb (http://www.jobweb.com) also offer interest inventories. Don't forget the help advisers at any two-year college can provide to target your interests. You'll find suggestions for Web sites related to specific careers at the end of each chapter in any *Top Careers in Two Years* volume.

Unlock Your Network

The next stop toward landing the perfect job is networking. The word may make you cringe. But networking isn't about putting on a suit, walking into a roomful of strangers, and pressing your business card on everyone. Networking is simply introducing yourself and exchanging job-related and other information that may prove helpful to one or both of you. That's what Susan Tinker-Muller did. Quite a few years ago, she struck up a conversation with a fellow passenger on her commuter train. Little did she know that the natural interest she expressed in the woman's accounts payable department would lead to news about a job opening there. Tinker-Muller's networking landed her an entry-level position in accounts payable with MTV Networks. She is now the accounts payable administrator.

Tinker-Muller's experience illustrates why networking is so important. Fully 80 percent of openings are *never* advertised, and more than half of all employees land their jobs through networking, according to the U.S. Bureau of Labor Statistics. That's 8 out of 10 jobs that you'll miss if you don't get out there and talk with people. And don't think you can bypass face-to-face conversations by posting your résumé on job sites like Monster.com and Hotjobs.com and then waiting for employers to contact you. That's so mid-1990s! Back then, tens of thousands, if not millions, of job seekers diligently posted their résumés on scores of sites. Then they sat back and waited . . . and waited . . . and waited. You get the idea. Big job sites like Monster and Hotjobs have their place, of course, but relying solely on an Internet job search is about as effective as throwing your résumé into a black hole.

Begin your networking efforts by making a list of people to talk to: teachers, classmates (and their parents), anyone you've worked with, neighbors, worship acquaintances, and anyone you've interned or volunteered with. You can also expand your networking opportunities through the student sections of industry associations (listed at the end of each chapter of *Top Careers in Two Years*); attending or volunteering at industry events, association conferences, career fairs; and through job-shadowing. Keep in mind that only rarely will any of the people on your list be in a position to offer you a job. But whether they know it or not, they probably know someone who knows someone who is. That's why your networking goal is not to ask for a job but the name of someone to talk with. Even when you network with an employer, it's wise to say something like, "You may not have any positions available, but might you know someone I could talk with to find out more about what it's like to work in this field?"

Also, keep in mind that networking is a two-way street. For instance, you may be talking with someone who has a job opening that isn't appropriate for you. If you can refer someone else to the employer, either person may well be disposed to help you someday in the future.

Dial-Up Help

Call your contacts directly, rather than e-mail them. (E-mails are too easy for busy people to ignore, even if they don't mean to.) Explain that you're a recent graduate in your field; that Mr. Jones referred you; and that you're wondering if you could stop by for 10 or 15 minutes at your contact's convenience to find out a little more about how the industry works. If you leave this message as a voicemail, note that you'll call back in a few days to follow up. If you reach your contact directly, expect that they'll say they're too busy at the moment to see you. Ask, "Would you mind if I check back in a couple of weeks?" Then jot down a note in your date book or set up a reminder in your computer calendar and call back when it's time. (Repeat this above scenario as needed, until you get a meeting.)

Once you have arranged to talk with someone in person, prep yourself. Scour industry publications for insightful articles; having up-to-date knowledge about industry trends shows your networking contacts that you're dedicated and focused. Then pull together questions about specific employers and suggestions that will set you apart from the job-hunting pack in your field. The more specific your questions (for instance, about one type of certification versus another), the more likely your contact will see you as an "insider," worthy of passing along to a potential employer. At the end of any networking meeting, ask for the name of someone else who might be able to help you further target your search.

Get a Lift

When you meet with a contact in person (as well as when you run into someone fleetingly), you need an "elevator speech." This is a summary of up to two minutes that introduces who you are, as well as your experience and goals. An elevator speech should be short enough to be delivered during an elevator ride with a potential employer from the ground level to a high floor. In it, it's helpful to show that 1) you know the business involved; 2) you know the company; 3) you're qualified (give your work and educational information); and 4) you're goal-oriented, dependable, and hardworking. You'll be surprised how much information you can include in two minutes. Practice this speech in front of a mirror until you have the key points down very well. It should sound natural though, and you should come across as friendly, confident, and assertive. Remember, good eye contact needs to be part of your presentation as well as your everyday approach when meeting prospective employers or leads.

Get Your Résumé Ready

In addition to your elevator speech, another essential job-hunting tool is your résumé. Basically, a résumé is a little snapshot of you in words, reduced to one 8½ x 11-inch sheet of paper (or, at most, two sheets). You need a résumé whether you're in high school, college, or the workforce, and whether you've never held a job or have had many.

At the top of your résumé should be your heading. This is your name, address, phone numbers, and your e-mail address, which can be a sticking point. E-mail addresses such as sillygirl@yahoo.com or drinkingbuddy @hotmail.com won't score you any points. In fact they're a turn-off. So if you dreamed up your address after a night on the town, maybe it's time to upgrade. (Similarly, these days potential employers often check Myspace sites, personal blogs, and Web pages. What's posted there has been known to cost candidates a job offer.)

The first section of your résumé is a concise Job Objective (e.g., "Entry-level agribusiness sales representative seeking a position with a leading dairy cooperative"). These days, with word-processing software, it's easy and smart to adapt your job objective to the position for which you're applying. An alternative way to start a résumé, which some recruiters prefer, is to re-work the Job Objective into a Professional Summary. A Professional Summary doesn't mention the position you're seeking, but instead focuses on your job strengths (e.g., "Entry-level agribusiness sales rep; strengths include background in feed, fertilizer, and related markets and ability to contribute as a member of a sales team"). Which is better? It's your call.

The body of a résumé typically starts with your Job Experience. This is a chronological list of the positions you've held (particularly the ones that will help you land the job you want). Remember: never, never any fudging. However, it is okay to include volunteer positions and internships on the chronological list, as long as they're noted for what they are.

Next comes your Education section. Note: It's acceptable to flip the order of your Education and Job Experience sections if you're still in high school or have gone straight to college and don't have significant work experience. Summarize the major courses in your degree area, any certifications you've achieved, relevant computer knowledge, special seminars, or other school-related experience that will distinguish you. Include your grade average if it's more than 3.0. Don't worry if you haven't finished your degree. Simply write that you're currently enrolled in your program (if you are).

In addition to these elements, other sections may include professional organizations you belong to and any work-related achievements, awards, or recognition you've received. Also, you can have a section for your interests, such as playing piano or soccer (and include any notable achievements regarding your interests, for instance, placed third in Midwest Regional Piano Competition). You should also note other special abilities, such as "Fluent in French" or "Designed own Web site." These sorts of activities will reflect well on you, whether or not they are job-related.

You can either include your references or simply note, "References upon Request." Be sure to ask your references permission to use their name and alert them to the fact that they may be contacted, before you include them on your résumé. For more information on résumé writing, check out Web sites such as http://www.resume.monster.com.

Craft Your Cover Letter

When you apply for a job either online or by mail, it's appropriate to include a cover letter. A cover letter lets you convey extra information about yourself that doesn't fit or isn't always appropriate in your résumé. For instance, in a cover letter, you can and should mention the name of anyone who referred you to the job. You can go into some detail about the reason you're a great match, given the job description. You also can address any questions that might be raised in the potential employer's mind (for instance, a gap in your résumé). Don't, however, ramble on. Your cover letter should stay focused on your goal: to offer a strong, positive impression of yourself and persuade the hiring manager that you're worth an interview. Your cover letter gives you a chance to stand out from the other applicants and sell yourself. In fact, 23 percent of hiring managers say a candidate's ability to relate his or her experience to the job at hand is a top hiring consideration, according to a Careerbuilder.com survey.

You can write a positive, yet concise cover letter in three paragraphs: An introduction containing the specifics of the job you're applying for; a summary of why you're a good fit for the position and what you can do for the company; and a closing with a request for an interview, contact information, and thanks. Remember to vary the structure and tone of your cover letter. For instance, don't begin every sentence with "I."

Ace Your Interview

Preparation is the key to acing any job interview. This starts with researching the company or organization you're interviewing with. Start with the firm, group, or agency's own Web site. Explore it thoroughly; read about their products and services, their history, and sales and marketing information.

Check out their news releases, links that they provide, and read up on or Google members of the management team to get an idea of what they may be looking for in their employees.

Sites such as http://www.hoovers.com enable you to research companies across many industries. Trade publications in any industry (such as *Food Industry News*, *Hotel Business*, and *Hospitality Technology*) are also available online or in hard copy at many college or public libraries. Don't forget to make a phone call to contacts you have in the organization to get an even better idea of the company culture.

Preparation goes beyond research, however. It includes practicing answers to common interview questions:

☞ *Tell me about yourself* (Don't talk about your favorite bands or your personal history; give a brief summary of your background and interest in the particular job area.)

☞ *Why do you want to work here?* (Here's where your research into the company comes into play; talk about the firm's strengths and products or services.)

☞ *Why should we hire you?* (Now is your chance to sell yourself as a dependable, trustworthy, effective employee.)

☞ *Why did you leave your last job?* (This is not a talk show. Keep your answer short; never bad-mouth a previous employer. You can always say something simply such as, "It wasn't a good fit, and I was ready for other opportunities.")

Rehearse your answers, but don't try to memorize them. Responses that are natural and spontaneous come across better. Trying to memorize exactly what you want to say is likely to both trip you up and make you sound robotic.

As for the actual interview, to break the ice, offer a few pleasant remarks about the day, a photo in the interviewer's office, or something else similar. Then, once the interview gets going, listen closely and answer the questions you're asked, versus making any other point that you want to convey. If you're unsure whether your answer was adequate, simply ask, "Did that answer the question?" Show respect, good energy, and enthusiasm, and be upbeat. Employers are looking for people who are enjoyable to be around, as well as good workers. Show that you have a positive attitude and can get along well with others by not bragging during the interview, overstating your experience, or giving the appearance of being too self-absorbed. Avoid one-word answers, but at the same time don't blather. If you're faced with a silence after giving your response, pause for a few seconds, and then ask, "Is there anything else you'd like me to add?" Never look at your watch or answer your cellphone during an interview.

Near the interview's end, the interviewer is likely to ask you if you have any questions. Make sure that you have a few prepared, for instance:

☞ *"Tell me about the production process."*

☞ *"What's your biggest short-term challenge?"*

☞ *"How have recent business trends affected the company?"*

☞ *"Is there anything else that I can provide you with to help you make your decision?"*

☞ *"When will you make your hiring decision?"*

During a first interview, never ask questions like, "What's the pay?" "What are the benefits?" or "How much vacation time will I get?"

Find the Right Look

Appropriate dressing and grooming is also essential to interviewing success. For business jobs and many other occupations, it's appropriate to come to an interview in a nice (not stuffy) suit. However, different fields have various dress codes. In the music business, for instance, "business casual" reigns for many jobs. This is a slightly modified look, where slacks and a jacket are just fine for a guy, and a nice skirt and blouse and jacket or sweater are acceptable for a woman. Dressing overly "cool" will usually backfire.

In general, watch all of the basics from the shoes on up (no sneakers or sandals, and no overly high heels or short skirts for women). Also avoid attention-getting necklines, girls. Keep jewelry and other "bling" to a minimum. Tattoos and body jewelry are becoming more acceptable, but if you can take out piercings (other than in your ear), you're better off. Similarly, unusual hairstyles or colors may bias an employer against you, rightly or wrongly. Make sure your hair is neat and acceptable (get a haircut?). Also go light on the makeup, self-tanning products, body scents, and other grooming agents. Don't wear a baseball cap or any other type of hat; and by all means, take off your sunglasses!

Beyond your physical appearance, you already know to be well bathed to minimize odor (leave your home early if you tend to sweat, so you can cool off in private), make good eye contact, smile, speak clearly using proper English, use good posture (don't slouch), offer a firm handshake, and arrive within five minutes of your interview. (If you're unsure of where you're going, "Mapquest" it and consider making a dry-run to the site so you won't be late.) First impressions can make or break your interview.

Remember Follow-Up

After your interview, send a thank you note. This thoughtful gesture will separate you from most of the other candidates. It demonstrates your ability to follow through, and it catches your prospective employer's attention one more time. In a 2005 Careerbuilder.com survey, nearly 15 percent of 650 hiring managers said they wouldn't hire someone who failed to send a thank you letter after the interview. Thirty-two percent say they would still consider the candidate, but would think less of him or her.

So do you hand write or e-mail the thank you letter? The fact is that format preferences vary. One in four hiring managers prefer to receive a thank you note in e-mail form only; 19 percent want the e-mail, followed up with a hard copy; 21 percent want a typed hard-copy only; and 23 percent prefer just a handwritten note. (Try to check with an assistant on the format your potential employer prefers.) Otherwise, sending an e-mail and a handwritten copy is a safe way to proceed.

Winning an Offer

There are no sweeter words to a job hunter than "We'd like to hire you." So naturally, when you hear them, you may be tempted to jump at the offer. *Don't.* Once an employer wants you, he or she will usually give you some time to make your decision and get any questions you may have answered. Now is the time to get specific about salary and benefits, and negotiate some of these points. If you haven't already done so, check out salary ranges for your position and area of the country on sites such as Payscale.com, Salary.com, and Salaryexpert.com (basic info is free; specific requests are not). Also, find out what sorts of benefits similar jobs offer. Then don't be afraid to negotiate in a diplomatic way. Asking for better terms is reasonable and expected. You may worry that asking the employer to bump up his offer may jeopardize your job, but handled intelligently, negotiating for yourself in fact may be a way to impress your future employer—and get a better deal for yourself.

After you've done all the hard work that successful job-hunting requires, you may be tempted to put your initiative into autodrive. However, the efforts you made to land your job-from clear communication to enthusiasm-are necessary now to pave your way to continued success. As Danielle Little, a human-resources assistant, says, "You must be enthusiastic and take the initiative. There is an urgency to prove yourself and show that you are capable of performing any and all related tasks. If your manager notices that you have potential, you will be given additional responsibilities, which will help advance your career." So do your best work on the job, and build your credibility. Your payoff will be career advancement and increased earnings.

Appendix B

Financial Aid

One major advantage of earning a two-year degree is that it is much less expensive than paying for a four-year school. Two years is naturally going to cost less than four, and two-year graduates enter the workplace and start earning a paycheck sooner than their four-year counterparts.

The latest statistics from the College Board show that average yearly total tuition and fees at a public two-year college is $2,191, compared to $5,491 at a four-year public college. That cost leaps to more than $21,000 on average for a year at a private four-year school.

With college costs relatively low, some two-year students overlook the idea of applying for financial aid at all. But the fact is, college dollars are available whether you're going to a trade school, community college, or university. About a third of all Pell Grants go to two-year public school students, and while two-year students receive a much smaller percentage of other aid programs, the funding is there for many who apply.

How Does Aid Work?

Financial aid comes in two basic forms: merit-based and need-based.

Merit-based awards are typically funds that recognize a particular talent or quality you may have, and they are given by private organizations, colleges, and the government. Merit-based awards range from scholarships for good writing to prizes for those who have shown promise in engineering. There are thousands of scholarships available for students who shine in academics, music, art, science, and more. Resources on how to get these awards are provided later in this chapter.

Need-based awards are given according to your ability to pay for college. In general, students from families that have less income and fewer assets receive more financial aid. To decide how much of this aid you qualify for, schools look at your family's income, assets, and other information regarding your finances. You provide this information on a financial aid form—usually the federal government's Free Application for Federal Student Aid (FAFSA). Based on the financial details you provide, the school of your choice calculates your Expected Family Contribution (EFC). This is the amount you are expected to pay toward your education each year.

Once your EFC is determined, a school uses this simple formula to figure out your financial aid package:

Cost of attendance at the school

– **Your EFC**

– **Other outside aid (private scholarships)**

= **Need**

Schools put together aid packages that meet that need using loans, work-study, and grants.

Know Your School

When applying to a school, it's a good idea to find out their financial aid policy and history. Read over the school literature or contact the financial aid office and find out the following:

✔ *Is the school accredited?* Schools that are not accredited usually do not offer as much financial aid and are not eligible for federal programs.

✔ *What is the average financial aid package at the school?* The typical award size may influence your decision to apply or not.

✔ *What are all the types of assistance available?* Check if the school offers federal, state, private, or institutional aid.

✔ *What is the school's loan default rate?* The default rate is the percentage of students who took out federal student loans and failed to repay them on time. Schools that have a high default rate are often not allowed to offer certain federal aid programs.

✔ *What are the procedures and deadlines for submitting financial aid?* Policies can differ from school to school.

✔ *What is the school's definition of satisfactory academic progress?* To receive financial aid, you have to maintain your academic performance. A school may specify that you keep up at least a C+ or B average to keep getting funding.

✔ *What is the school's job placement rate?* The job placement rate is the percentage of students who find work in their field of study after graduating.

You'll want a school with a good placement rate so you can earn a good salary that may help you pay back any student loans you have.

Be In It to Win It

The key to getting the most financial aid possible is filling out the forms, and you have nothing to lose by applying. Most schools require that you file the FAFSA, which is *free* to submit, and you can even do it online. For more information on the FAFSA, visit the Web site at http://www.fafsa.ed.gov. If you have any trouble with the form, you can call 1-800-4-FED-AID for help.

To receive aid using the FAFSA, you must submit the form soon after January 1 prior to the start of your school year. A lot of financial aid is delivered on a first-come, first-served basis, so be sure to apply on time.

Filing for aid will require some work to gather your financial information. You'll need details regarding your assets and from your income tax forms, which include the value of all your bank accounts and investments. The form also asks if you have other siblings in college, the age of your parents, or if you have children. These factors can determine how much aid you receive.

Three to four weeks after you submit the FAFSA, you receive a document called the Student Aid Report (SAR). The SAR lists all the information you provided in the FAFSA and tells you how much you'll be expected to contribute toward school, or your Expected Family Contribution (EFC). It's important to review the information on the SAR carefully and make any corrections right away. If there are errors on this document, it can affect how much financial aid you'll receive.

The Financial Aid Package

Using information on your SAR, the school of your choice calculates your need (as described earlier) and puts together a financial aid package. Aid packages are often built with a combination of loans, grants, and work-study. You may also have won private scholarships that will help reduce your costs.

Keep in mind that aid awarded in the form of loans has to be paid back with interest just like a car loan. If you don't pay back according to agreed upon terms, you can go into *default*. Default usually occurs if you've missed payments for 180 days. Defaulted loans are often sent to collection agencies, which can charge costly fees and even take money owed out of your wages. Even worse, a defaulted loan is a strike on your credit history. If you have a negative credit history, lenders may deny you a mortgage, car loan, or other personal loan. There's also financial incentive for paying back on time—many lenders will give a 1 percent discount or more for students who make consecutive timely payments. The key is not to borrow more than you can afford. Know exactly how much your monthly payments will be on a loan when it comes due and estimate if those monthly payments will fit in your future budget. If you ever do run into trouble with loan payments, don't hesitate to contact your lender and see if you can come up with a new payment arrangement—lenders want to help you pay rather than see you go into default. If you have more than one loan, look into loan consolidation, which can lower overall monthly payments and sometimes lock in interest rates that are relatively low.

The Four Major Sources of Aid

U.S. Government Financial Aid

The federal government is the biggest source of financial aid. To find all about federal aid programs, visit http://www.studentaid.fed.gov or call 1-800-4-FED-AID with any questions. Download the free brochure *Funding Education Beyond High School*, which tells you all the details on federal programs. To get aid from federal programs you must be a regular student working toward a degree or certificate in an eligible program. You also have to have a high school diploma or equivalent, be a U.S. citizen or eligible noncitizen and have a valid Social Security number (check http://www.ssa.gov for info). If you are a male aged 18–25, you have to register for the Selective Service. (Find out more about that requirement at http://www.sss.gov or call 1-847-688-6888.) You must also certify that you are not in default on a student loan and that you will use your federal aid only for educational purposes.

Some specifics concerning federal aid programs can change a little each year, but the major programs are listed here and the fundamentals stay the same from year to year. (Note that amounts you receive generally depend on your enrollment status—whether it be full-time or part-time.)

Pell Grant

For students demonstrating significant need, this award has been ranging between $400 and $4,050. The size of a Pell grant does not depend on how much other aid you receive.

Supplemental Educational Opportunity Grant (SEOG)

Again for students with significant need, this award ranges from $100 to $4,000 a year. The size of the SEOG can be reduced according to how much other aid you receive.

Work-Study

The Federal Work-Study Program provides jobs for students showing financial need. The program encourages community service and work related to a student's course of study. You earn at least minimum wage and are paid at least once a month. Again, funds must be used for educational expenses.

Perkins Loans

With a low interest rate of 5 percent, this program lets students who can document the need borrow up to $4,000 a year.

Stafford Loans

These loans are available to all students regardless of need. However, students with need receive *subsidized* Staffords, which do not accrue interest while you're in school or in deferment. Students without need can take *unsubsidized* Staffords, which do accrue interest while you are in school or in deferment. Interest rates vary but can go no higher than 8.25 percent. Loan amounts vary too, according to what year of study you're in and whether you are financially dependent on your parents or not. Students defined as independent of their parents can borrow much more. (Students who have their own kids are also defined as independent. Check the exact qualifications for independent and dependent status on the federal government Web site http://www.studentaid.fed.gov.)

PLUS Loans

These loans for parents of dependent students are also available regardless of need. Parents with good credit can borrow up to the cost of attendance minus any other aid received. Interest rates are variable but can go no higher than 9 percent.

Tax Credits

Depending on your family income, qualified students can take federal tax deductions for education with maximums ranging from $1,500 to $2,000.

AmeriCorps

This program provides full-time educational awards in return for community service work. You can work before, during, or after your postsecondary education and use the funds either to pay current educational expenses or to repay federal student loans. Americorps participants work assisting teachers in Head Start, helping on conservation projects, building houses for the homeless, and doing other good works. For more information, visit http://www.AmeriCorps.gov

State Financial Aid

All states offer financial aid, both merit-based and need-based. Most states use the FAFSA to determine eligibility, but you'll have to contact your state's higher education agency to find out the exact requirements. You can get contact information for your state at http://www.bcol02.ed.gov/Programs/EROD/org_list.cfm. Most of the state aid programs are available only if you

study at a school in the state where you reside. Some states are very gener-
ous, especially if you're attending a state college or university. California's
Cal Grant program gives needy state residents free tuition at in-state public
universities.

School-Sponsored Financial Aid

The school you attend may offer its own loans, grants, and work programs.
Many have academic- or talent-based scholarships for top-performing students. Some two-year programs offer cooperative education opportunities
where you combine classroom study with off-campus work related to your
major. The work gives you hands-on experience and some income, ranging
from $2,500 to $15,000 per year depending on the program. Communicate with your school's financial aid department and make sure you're applying for the most aid you can possibly get.

Private Scholarships

While scholarships for students heading to four-year schools may be more
plentiful, there are awards for the two-year students. Scholarships reward
students for all sorts of talent—academic, artistic, athletic, technical, scientific, and more. You have to invest time hunting for the awards that you
might qualify for. The Internet now offers many great scholarship search services. Some of the best ones are:

> The College Board (http://www.collegeboard.com/pay)
>
> FastWeb! (http://www.fastweb.monster.com)
>
> MACH25 (http://www.collegenet.com)
>
> Scholarship Research Network (http://www.srnexpress.com)
>
> SallieMae's College Answer (http://www.collegeanswer.com)

Note: Be careful of scholarship-scam services that charge a fee for finding you awards but end up giving you nothing more than a few leads that
you could have gotten for free with a little research on your own. Check out
the Federal Trade Commission's Project ScholarScam (http://www.ftc.gov/
bcp/conline/edcams/scholarship).

In your hunt for scholarship dollars, be sure to look into local community organizations (the Elks Club, Lions Club, PTA, etc.), local corpora-
tions, employers (your employer or your parents' may offer tuition
assistance), trade groups, professional associations (National Electrical
Contractors Association, etc.), clubs (Boy Scouts, Girl Scouts, Distributive
Education Club of America, etc.), heritage organizations (Italian, Japanese,

Chinese, and other groups related to ethnic origin), church groups, and minority assistance programs.

Once you find awards you qualify for, you have to put in the time applying. This usually means filling out an application, writing a personal statement, and gathering recommendations.

General Scholarships

A few general scholarships for students earning two-year degrees are

Coca-Cola Scholars Foundation, Inc.
Coca-Cola offers 350 thousand-dollar scholarships (http://www.coca colascholars.org) per year specifically for students attending two-year institutions.

Phi Theta Kappa (PTK)
This organization is the International Honor Society of the Two-Year College. PTK is one of the sponsors of the All-USA Academic Team program, which annually recognizes 60 outstanding two-year college students (http://scholarships.ptk.org). First, Second, and Third Teams, each consisting of 20 members, are selected. The 20 First Team members receive stipends of $2,500 each. All 60 members of the All-USA Academic Team and their colleges receive extensive national recognition through coverage in *USA TODAY*. There are other great scholarships for two-year students listed on this Web site.

Hispanic Scholarship Fund (HSF)
HSF's High School Scholarship Program (http://www.hsf.net/scholar ship/programs/hs.php) is designed to assist high school students of Hispanic heritage obtain a college degree. It is available to graduating high school seniors who plan to enroll full-time at a community college during the upcoming academic year. Award amounts range from $1,000 to $2,500.

The Military
All branches of the military offer tuition dollars in exchange for military service. You have to decide if military service is for you. The Web site http://www.myfuture.com attempts to answer any questions you might have about military service.

Lower Your Costs

In addition to getting financial aid, you can reduce college expenses by being a money-smart student. Here are some tips.

Use Your Campus

Schools offer perks that some students never take advantage of. Use the gym. Take in a school-supported concert or movie night. Attend meetings and lectures with free refreshments.

Flash Your Student ID

Students often get discounts at movies, museums, restaurants, and stores. Always be sure to ask if there is a lower price for students and carry your student ID with you at all times. You can often save 10 to 20 percent on purchases.

Budget Your Funds

Writing a budget of your income and expenses can help you be a smart spender. Track what you buy on a budget chart. This awareness will save you dollars.

Share Rides

Commuting to school or traveling back to your hometown? Check and post on student bulletin boards for ride shares.

Buy Used Books

Used textbooks can cost half as much as new. Check your campus bookstore for deals and also try http://www.eCampus.com and http://www.bookcentral.com

Put Your Credit Card in the Freezer

That's what one student did to stop overspending. You can lock your card away any way you like, just try living without the ease of credit for awhile. You'll be surprised at the savings.

A Two-Year Student's Financial Aid Package

Minnesota State Colleges and Universities provides this example of how a two-year student pays for college. Note how financial aid reduces his out-of-pocket cost to about $7,000 per year.

Jeremy's Costs for One Year

Jeremy is a freshman at a two-year college in the Minnesota. He has a sister in college, and his parents own a home but have no other significant savings. His family's income: $42,000.

College Costs for One Year

Tuition	$3,437
Fees	$388
Estimated room and board*	$7,200
Estimated living expenses**	$6,116
Total cost of attendance	*$17,141*

Jeremy's Financial Aid

Federal grants (does not require repayment)	$2,800
Minnesota grant (does not require repayment)	$676
Work-study earnings	$4,000
Student loan (requires repayment)	$2,625
Total financial aid	*$10,101*

Total cost to Jeremy's family — ***$7,040***

* Estimated cost reflecting apartment rent rate and food costs. The estimates are used to calculate the financial aid. If a student lives at home with his or her parents, the actual cost could be much less, although the financial aid amounts may remain the same.

** This is an estimate of expenses including transportation, books, clothing, and social activities.

Index

A

aerospace technician, 19–27
  ethics, 22
  feats by, 26
  financial aid, 27
  hands-on work of, 25
  international cooperation between, 20
  opportunity for young workers as, 24
  tasks of, 21–22
  training, 23–24
air traffic controller, 45–53
  communication on internet, 52
  financial aid, 53
  multitasking as, 51
  physical/psychological health of, 48
  politics facing, 50
  tasks of, 47–48
  teamwork of, 46
  training, 49–50
aircraft mechanic, 28–36
  computer knowledge needed by, 33
  financial aid, 35–36
  large v. small airport employment of, 29
  specialization, 31
  tasks of, 30–31
  training, 32–33
  travel opportunity for, 34
American Chemical Society, 73
American Society for Quality, 5–6
associate's degree programs, 8. *See also* training; two-year degree program
  aerospace technician, 26
  air traffic controller, 52
  aircraft mechanic, 35
  chemical technician, 78
  cost of, 118–119
  distribution manager, 17–18
  dock supervisor, 44
  laser technician, 86
  machinist, 61
  microelectronics technician, 94
  plastics technician, 102
  robotics technician, 69
  salary rankings among, xiii

B

benefits, 110
breaking in
  as aerospace technician, 23
  to air traffic controller, 49
  to aircraft mechanics, 32
  as chemical technician, 75
  to distribution management, 14
  as dock supervisor, 41
  as laser technician, 82–83
  as machinist, 58
  as microelectronics technician, 90–91
  as plastics technician, 99
  to quality management, 5
  as robotics technician, 66

C

career connections
  aerospace technician, 26
  air traffic controller, 52
  aircraft mechanic, 35
  chemical technician, 78
  distribution manager, 17
  dock supervisor, 44
  laser technician, 86
  machinist, 61
  microelectronics technician, 93
  plastics technician, 102
  quality manager, 8

robotics technician, 69
certification
    avionics, 32
    keeping valid, 31
    voluntary, 5
chemical technician, 71–78
    design by, 72
    financial aid, 78
    lab positions for, 77
    manual/mental dexterity of, 74
    salary of, 72, 76
    tasks of, 73–74
    training, 75
college expenses, 117–118
communication, 105
community service, 115
computer
    chip design, 89
    enhanced radar, 50
    knowledge, 33
    skills, ix
continuing education, xii
cover letter, 107
cutting-edge work, 63–64

D
deregulation, 12
design
    chemical technician doing, 72
    computer chip, 89
    template, 81
distance learning, xiv
distribution manager, 10–18
    financial aid, 18
    industry trends understood by, 13–14
    motivation from, 14
    purchasing agent rise to, 11
    statistics, 17
    tangible results of, 16
    tasks of, 12–13
    training, 15
dock supervisor, 37–44
    big picture seen by, 40
    changing technology faced by, 42
    financial aid, 44
    leadership, 38

tasks of, 39–40
training, 41–42
union environment of, 43
dress, 109

E
education. *See also* continuing education
    awards, 115
    continuing, xii
    distance, xiv
    impact on future from, 101
EFC. *See* expected family contribution
electromechanical workers. *See* Robotics
    technician
e-mail
    addresses, 106
    communication, 105
    thank you letter by, 110
expected family contribution (EFC), 111,
    113

F
FAA (Federal Aviation Administration),
    30, 32, 47
FAFSA (Free Application for Federal
    Student Aid), xii, 111, 113
Federal Aviation Administration. *See* FAA
financial aid, 111–119
    aerospace technician, 27
    aircraft mechanic, 35–36
    air traffic controller, 53
    chemical technician, 78
    distribution manager, 18
    dock supervisors, 44
    example of, 118–119
    laser technician, 86
    machinist, 61
    microelectronics technician, 94
    package, 113–114
    plastics technician, 102
    quality manager, 8
    research, 112
    robotics technician, 69–70
    school-sponsored, 116
    state, 115–116

statistics, 119
U.S. government, 114–115
follow-up, 109–110
four-year degree program
    expense of, x, 111
    unemployment after, xiii
Free Application for Federal Student Aid.
    See FAFSA
future
    aerospace technicians, 24
    aircraft mechanics, 33
    air traffic controllers, 50
    aviation's, 29
    chemical technicians, 76
    distribution managers, 15
    dock supervisors, 42
    education's impact on, 101
    laser technicians, 83
    machinists, 59
    microelectronics technicians, 91
    plastics industry affecting, 97
    plastics technicians, 100
    quality managers, 3, 6
    robotics technicians, 67

G
GIS (global information system), 15
global information system. *See* GIS
Global Positioning System. *See* GPS
government
    deregulation, 12
    regulation, 3, 11
GPS (Global Positioning System), 15

H
hands-on experience, xiv

I
industry trends, 13–14
international Space Station, 20–21, 26
Internet
    air traffic controller communication
        on, 52
    classes via, xiv
    reliance on, 104

skills, ix
internship, xiv, 66, 75
interview
    acing, 107–109
    aerospace technician, 25
    aircraft mechanic, 34
    air traffic controller, 51
    chemical technician, 77
    distribution manager, 16
    dock supervisor, 43
    laser technician, 85
    machinist, 60
    microelectronics technician, 92
    plastics technician, 101
    preparation, 105
    quality manager, 7
    robotics technician, 68
    success, 109

J
job seeking tips
    aerospace technician, 26
    aircraft mechanic, 35
    air traffic controller, 52
    chemical technician, 76
    distribution manager, 17
    dock supervisor, 42
    eye contact, 106
    laser technician, 84
    machinist, 59
    microelectronics technician, 93
    plastics technician, 100
    quality manager, 8
    robotics technician, 69
job stability, ix, 59

L
laser technician, 79–86
    danger to, 82
    financial aid, 86
    power welded by, 84
    problem solving skills of, 85
    tasks of, 81–82
    tools of, 80
    training, 83

M

machinist, 54–61
  financial aid, 61
  job stability for, 59
  quality control by, 57
  software programs for, 60
  tasks of, 56–57
  tools used by, 55
  training, 58
management
  key of, 40
  principals of, 15
  supply-chain, x, 16
  team, 4
manager
  distribution, 10–18
  quality, 1–9
mechanic, aircraft, 28–36
microelectronics technician, 87–94
  blend of skill sets for, 90
  financial aid, 94
  guiding law for, 93
  practical science employed by, 88
  sterile working environment of, 92
  tasks of, 89–90
  training, 91

N

NASA (National Aeronautics and Space
    Administration), 20–25
National Aeronautics and Space
    Administration. *See* NASA
networking, 105
9/11, 24, 30, 34, 47

O

Occupational Outlook Handbook, 100
on-the-job inspector. *See* quality manager

P

photonics technology, 80–81
plastics technician, 95–102
  financial aid, 102
  inexhaustible opportunity for, 101
  international opportunity for, 96
  patience needed to be, 98

tasks of, 97–98
  training, 99
public safety, 51
purchasing agent, 11

Q

qualifications
  aerospace technician, 22
  aircraft mechanic, 31
  air traffic controller, 48
  chemical technician, 74
  distribution manager, 13–14
  dock supervisor, 39
  laser technician, 82
  machinist, 57
  microelectronics technician, 90
  quality manager, 4–5
  robotics technician, 65
quality control, 57
quality manager, 1–9
  financial aid, 8
  management team member of, 4
  professional groups for, 5
  quality technician supervised by, 7
  tasks of, 3–4
  training, 6
  trans-industrial skills of, 2–3
quality technician, 7

R

radar, computer-enhanced, 50
regulation, 3, 11
related careers
  aerospace technician, 27
  air traffic controller, 53
  chemical technician, 78
  distribution manager, 18
  dock supervisor, 44
  laser technician, 86
  machinist, 61
  microelectronics technician, 94
  plastics technician, 102
  quality manager, 9
  robotics technician, 70
research
  financial aid, 112

interview, 107–108
team nature of, xi
résumé
    adding credibility to, 75
    building, 14
    creation, 106
robotics technician, 62–70
    cutting-edge work carried out by,
        63–64
    ethics, 68
    financial aid, 69–70
    job security for, 67
    tasks of, 64–65
    training, 66

S
salary
    aerospace technicians, 20
    aircraft mechanics, 29
    air traffic controllers, 46
    associate's degree programs ranking of,
        xiii
    chemical technicians, 72, 76
    distribution managers, 11
    dock supervisors, 38
    laser technicians, 80
    machinists, 55
    microelectronics technicians, 88
    negotiation, 110
    plastics technicians, 96
    quality managers, 2
    robotics technicians, 63
SallieMae, xii
scholarships
    forms of, 111–112
    general, 117
    private, 116–117
Six Sigma, 2, 5
skilled labor shortage, 39
software programs, 60
SpaceTEC, xi, 21, 24–25
specialization, xii, 31
statistics
    aerospace technician, 20
    aircraft mechanic, 29, 33
    air traffic controller, 46
    chemical technician, 72

distribution manager, 11, 17
dock supervisor, 38
hiring, 107
labor, 104
laser technician, 80
machinist, 55
microelectronics technician, 88
plastics technician, 96
quality manager, 2
robotics technician, 63
tuition, xii, 119
two-year degree program, x
success
    aerospace technician, 22
    aircraft mechanic, 31
    air traffic controller, 48
    career, 103–110
    chemical technician, 74
    distribution manager, 13
    dock supervisor, 40
    interview, 109
    laser technician, 82
    machinist, 57
    microelectronics technician, 90
    plastics technician, 98
    quality manager, 4
    robotics technician, 65
supply-chain management, x, 16

T
technician
    aerospace, 19–27
    chemical, 71–78
    laser, 79–86
    microelectronics, 87–94
    plastics, 95–102
    quality, 7
    robotics, 62–70
technology, 42
template design, 81
tools
    career success, 103–110
    laser technicians, 80
    machinist, 55
Top Careers in Two Years, 103–104
training
    aerospace technician, 23–24

aircraft mechanic, 32–33
air traffic controller, 49–50
chemical technician, 75
continuing, 84
distribution manager, 15
dock supervisor, 41–42
laser technician, 83
machinist, 58
microelectronics technician, 91
plastics technician, 99
quality manager, 6
robotics technician, 66
targeted technical, xi
travel opportunity, 12, 34
troubleshooting, 85
tuition statistics, xii, 119
two-year degree program
    considerations, 6, 15, 24, 33, 42, 50,
        58–59, 67, 76, 83–84, 91, 99
    cost example, 118
    pro's of, 111
    statistics, x
typical workday
    aerospace technicians, 23

aircraft mechanics, 32
air traffic controllers, 49
chemical technicians, 75
distribution managers, 14
dock supervisors, 41
laser technicians, 82
machinists, 57
microelectronics technicians, 90
plastics technicians, 98
quality managers, 5
robotics technicians, 66

U
union environment, 43

V
voluntary certification, 5

W
Web sites, x, xii, 49, 52, 55–56, 73, 104,
        107–110, 113–118
work-study, 114–115